MIND ON THE RUN

A Bipolar Chronicle

dottie pacharis

Idyll Arbor, Inc.

39129 264th Ave SE, Enumclaw, WA 98022 (360) 825-7797

Cover design: Mary Hearn
Idyll Arbor editor: Lynne Mallinson

ISBN: 9781882883912

Printed in the United States of America

Library of Congress Cataloging-in-Publication Data

Pacharis, Dottie.
  Mind on the run : a bipolar chronicle / Dottie Pacharis.
    p. cm.
  ISBN 978-1-882883-91-2 (alk. paper)
  1. Baker, Scott C., d. 2007--Mental health. 2. Manic-depressive persons--Virginia--Biography. 3. Manic-depressive illness. I. Title.
  RC516.P33 2011
  616.89'50092--dc22
  [B]

                                          2011007067

MIND ON THE RUN

In Memory of
Scott C. Baker
January 18, 1967 – February 5, 2007

Dedicated to his wife, Sarah, and his siblings,
Kathy, Jeff (Buddy), Tricia,
Chris, and Jodie

Contents

FOREWORD

The story that follows documents the events of a young man living and dying with an unpredictable illness that affected every person around him. You'll read of hopefulness when solutions and safety nets seemed in place. You'll read of frustration and disappointment when everything falls apart because one person in a position of authority couldn't understand the illness, the patient's history, and the toll it took on Scott Baker and his family.

I had the privilege to be Scott's pastor from 1998 until 2003, when he moved his membership to a church closer to his new home. Congregation members often described him as charismatic, energetic, enthusiastic, generous, intelligent, exciting but unpredictable, a successful businessman, and having a heart of gold, willing to help anyone.

As you read this well-documented journey of a man and those who loved him, you may find yourself filled with frustration and helplessness similar to the emotions of Scott's family. When I read the manuscript, I was reminded of my own emotions and sense of helplessness. I was grateful I had a medical background in nursing and had worked at St. Elizabeth's Mental Hospital in Washington, DC.

During the one manic stage with which I was closely connected, phone calls or knocks on the door would come at any time — day or night — and no amount of persuasion would change or alter Scott's manic agenda. Occasional outbursts during a meeting or worship service required explanation on my part. As his outbursts and eccentric behavior grew more frequent and more public, I had many opportunities to educate my congregation about mental illness. Scott's increasingly frequent outbursts and demonstrations of unsafe and poor judgment became more difficult to explain, especially when an hour before or an hour later, Scott's behavior and conversation appeared normal.

— • —

I write to honor Scott's memory and faith. I write to honor Scott's wife, Sarah, who loved him and did all she could to support him throughout his erratic, frightening illness. I write to honor Scott's family, who had resources most people do not have. This supportive family tried every possible means of averting Scott's final choice. I watched them change family and work schedules to be there for him. I watched them develop a network along the East Coast to keep him safe. I admired them for their creativity, diligence, and perseverance.

My prayer is that the story Scott's mother shares with us here will help those in authority to better understand the need for legal and medical directives that address individuals who can't follow medical advice due to temporary mental situations caused by bipolar conditions. My prayer is that all who read this story of one family's continual battles with existing laws will join our effort to find more compassionate and workable laws that both honor the individual's rights and provide families with appropriate, personalized plans for care. The result will be peace of mind and safe, effective medical care. My final prayer is that we, as a society, will continue to support research on how to effectively intervene while providing better care for all those involved with every mental illnesses.

Rev. Kathleen Monge, R.N.
Pastor in the Virginia Conference, United Methodist Church

Acknowledgments

To Jeanne Butzer, Roz Clark, Zimmie Goings, Joan Gordon, Stuart Pagel, and Joe Stehr for their editing assistance.

Special thanks to Tom Poland, journalist and author, for his professional manuscript assessment and editing assistance. Tom is an adjunct professor in the University of South Carolina's College of Mass Communications and Information Studies and an evening programs instructor of creative writing at Midlands Technical College in Columbia, South Carolina.

Many thanks to Scotty's high school girlfriend, Lorie Kirby Knowlton, for her friendship and support of this book to honor Scotty.

And to my husband, George, for allowing me to put my life on hold and devote two years to writing this book, for tolerating my many mood swings as I relived Scotty's illness and struggled to accurately record it on paper, for reading the manuscript more times than I can remember, for providing valuable feedback and suggestions, for his support throughout Scotty's illness, and for his continued support and assistance in writing this book.

WHY THIS BOOK?

This book chronicles my family's tragedy — the life and death of Scott C. Baker, known to us as "Scotty." It's the story of a suicide that proper treatment would have prevented. It's a story of our efforts to help Scotty through five major, prolonged bipolar manic episodes.

It's also an account of our family's experience with the inequities of this country's mental health care system, a system that takes hubris-like pride in protecting the individual rights of mentally ill people. In a classic case of overkill, the system's stringent shielding prevents families from getting loved ones timely, humane treatment. By allowing Scotty to go untreated for long periods, the system failed Scotty and left his family with the devastating shell of a severely ill man.

I always thought that if I outlived Scotty, I would write a book about his sad bipolar world. I wanted the book to pay tribute to him and all he endured. I wanted to write it for other families dealing with the same circumstances we coped with for more than thirteen years. My hope is that these families will be as outraged at our failed mental health care system as we were. My hope is they will join advocacy groups and get involved to change this country's laws governing the treatment of mental illness.

And so, I write this book with love and honor for Scotty, remembering him in all his well days, and those other days when he suffered so. I hope this book will help those unfamiliar with mental illness to realize that these people are not nuts, crazy, mad, or wacko — words I frequently hear used to describe the mentally ill. They have a brain disorder, they are ill, and like people with any other illness, they need medical treatment.

Much of this book chronicles Scotty's five manic episodes and what our family endured attempting to help him get treatment and recover. Most of the people you will meet on these pages are Scotty's immediate family and friends: his wife, Sarah; his sisters and brothers, Kathy, Jeff (Buddy), Tricia, Chris, and Jodie; his cousin, Sue, and her husband, Mike. You'll meet his employee, Joe, my husband, George, and me, Dottie, Scotty's mother for his last 30 years. You'll visit many places up and down the East Coast. So much happened between Scotty and us, before, in between, and afterwards that this book cannot hold it all. The incidents you read about here speak to just a part of the troubled times throughout his illness.

1. SAD JOURNEY

"You know, my mother loved flowers. I sure wish she could see all the pretty flowers that people brought her."

Words from a little boy. Little did I know that day the impact this child would have on my life — the little eight-year-old boy standing next to his mother's casket, talking about her flowers. That's how I met Scotty.

That was the beginning of Scotty's story as I know it, the beginning of *Mind on the Run*, his journey through elation and depression, my sentimental journey.

I knew his dad. We worked together and I went, along with others, to the funeral home to show our sympathy and compassion for him and his family during that tragic time. It was a difficult turning of a page in his life. His wife committed suicide and thus ended her struggles with severe depression and alcoholism. Now it was up to Scotty's dad to carry on with the care, nurture, and tending of four children.

I came to know Scotty's father later. Clovis Millican Baker, "Toby" to friends and family. Toby, a retired Navy Supply Corps officer, and I worked for a large financial institution in Washington, DC. We became friends, and over time our friendship turned into love.

Two and a half years after meeting Scotty at the funeral home, I married Toby. Scotty was now 10 years old. He had two sisters and a brother: Kathy, 18; Tricia, 13; and Jeff (Buddy), 17. I had two children from a previous marriage: a son, Chris, 11 and a daughter, Jodie, eight. Our new combined family of eight settled into a five-bedroom home in Springfield, Virginia, just down the street from where the Baker family had previously lived.

Soon after our marriage, Toby adopted my two children and we became known throughout the neighborhood as "the Baker Bunch." Two full-time careers and a family of six children between the ages of eight and 18 presented a challenge to all of us. Life in the Baker household was hectic, to say the least.

The older kids, Kathy and Buddy, were away at college during the school year and came home during the summer months. Our neighborhood had elementary, middle, and high schools within walking distance of our house, so the four younger kids walked to their respective schools. All four were very involved in school activities and played sports, but Scotty stood out, having a special drive about him to do more than just be a little boy and enjoy his childhood.

A boy in high gear always looking to see what was next — that was Scotty. His million-dollar smile, sense of humor, outgoing personality, and energy surpassed anything I'd ever seen. He captured my heart with his charm and was easy to love. He praised my cooking and his favorite meals. He was one of those kids who endeared himself to everyone.

Scholastically, Scotty was in a class all his own. Straight A's throughout elementary, middle, and high school were the norm, with little effort on his part. I rarely saw him study. He was gifted and by far the smartest of all six kids. Life did not challenge him — not yet. He was gregarious and a perpetual seeker, searching each day for new opportunities or new things to think about. Often, he found them.

Scotty became an entrepreneur at a young age. The weekend lemonade stand, a Krispy Kreme doughnut route, and delivering the daily newspaper on his bicycle became moneymakers for him. At age 12, he convinced the manager of a fast food restaurant in the local mall to hire him to chop lettuce and tomatoes after school and on weekends, no doubt lying about his age to get the job.

Scotty's siblings all played soccer. He played for a short time in a neighborhood league, but since no money could be made playing, he trained and became a soccer referee, working three to four games a weekend, earning $20 a game. Scotty even refereed adult games, never letting any outspoken adult players intimidate him.

Much of his referee earnings funded his love for bicycles. He always owned the latest and greatest bicycle on the market. If he tired of one, he sold it for a profit and purchased a new one. Scotty possessed natural talent for making money even as a kid.

At 13, Scotty cultivated a friendship with the owner of the bike shop in the local mall and convinced the owner to hire him part-time. With his outgoing personality, love of sales, and extensive bicycle knowledge, he soon sold more bikes than the owner. Backed by his impressive sales record, Scotty approached the owner a few months later and negotiated a commission on each bike sold, in addition to his part-time salary.

By 14, Scotty took charge of the store at times. That's how comfortable and impressed the owner was with Scotty's management and customer relationships.

Graduating from high school at the top of his class and voted "Most Likely to Succeed," Scotty was anxious to move on to college. James Madison University in Harrisonburg, Virginia, granted him early acceptance. Four very quick years later, during an unseasonably late snowstorm in May 1989, Scotty graduated with honors and an accounting degree. He received a job offer and began his career with what was then a "Big Ten" accounting firm in Washington, DC.

Before joining what he viewed as the "DC rat race," Scotty treated himself to a European vacation. He joined college friends on a one-month trip to Europe, traveling by train on a Eurail pass and staying at youth hostels. Money he earned at his part-time job waiting tables at a restaurant near the campus funded his trip. Only Scotty could describe his travel adventures so delightfully. We envied his travels and the things he saw.

During his second year with the firm, Scotty was chosen to participate in the Loaned Executives Program for the United Way in the DC area. Each year, community-minded employers lend key personnel to United Way as full-time fundraisers for its annual campaign. These executives use their talents and skills to develop successful campaigns in companies and organizations throughout the Washington metropolitan area.

This campaign sparked Scotty's first interest in philanthropy. He volunteered for Big Brothers of America. He found the United Way work so rewarding that he considered changing careers, but the limited non-profit earning capacity deterred him. He settled for displaying the many letters of commendation he received from his employer and United Way for his volunteer service.

On one hand, he had his business interests, and on the other, his romantic interests. One beautiful girl after another frequented our home. Here today and gone tomorrow was his dating philosophy, so I never let myself get attached to them. One girl, however, transcended his philosophy.

Scotty met Sarah Murray, a 19-year-old student at Marymount University in Arlington, Virginia, through a mutual friend. She modeled professionally in high school and was stunning. Sarah was different, and Scotty fell in love with her almost immediately. They married in August 1993. Sarah's parents loved Scotty and encouraged the marriage even though Sarah and Scotty had dated for less than a year.

Happy-go-lucky, not a care in the world, Scotty enjoyed each day to the fullest, viewing it as an opportunity to make a difference in the lives of others. No matter what the task, he made it fun for himself and entertaining for those around him. Life was good.

Married to a beautiful girl, climbing the ladder of success, an avenue of golden happiness lay ahead. Five months later in December 1993, disaster struck. Without warning, Scotty changed, becoming weird, maniacal, out-of-control, psychotic. In January 1994, Scotty's diagnosis came in — he was bipolar.

Sarah, young and shocked, stayed with Scotty five months. Unable to accept a husband with mental illness, her parents encouraged her to move back home and file for divorce. They, too, could not handle the stigma of a mentally ill son-in-law.

We moved on without Sarah, trying to fathom what had plunged Scotty into his disturbing world. His diagnosis brought two words into our lives, words as destructive as a runaway train: bipolar disorder.

Those words jangle the nerves, as though the world has turned upside down, and that's the truth. The disease unleashes a mind on the run that turns life topsy-turvy. I knew nothing about mental illness and sought information and guidance from the National Alliance on Mental Illness (NAMI). NAMI defines bipolar disorder, also known as manic-depressive disorder, as

> a complex medical illness of the brain involving episodes of serious mania and depression. It often runs in families. Genetic factors may create a predisposition in some people, and life stresses may trigger the onset of symptoms.
>
> Your chances of getting bipolar disorder are higher if your parents or siblings have the disorder. It's a lifelong illness with recurring episodes, and recovery between episodes is often poor. In the United States alone, over 10 million people have bipolar disorder.

According to NAMI, "bipolar can occur at any time but usually begins before age 35. People between the ages of 15 and 25 years have the highest risk of developing this disorder. However, the delay between the first signs and symptoms of the disorder and proper diagnosis and treatment is often 10 years."

Although Scotty was 27 before finally being diagnosed, I recall some fleeting signs of mania during his teenage and college years. At the time I, like others, thought nothing of them. We dismissed them as different behavior due to his very outgoing personality.

This horrible illness took Scotty on a 13-year roller coaster ride. It eventually robbed him of his outgoing personality, his self-esteem, and his self-confidence. It destroyed his short-term memory and his thought processes, rendering him unemployable. The illness weighed heavily on two marriages, neither of which survived. His best friend became his dog.

People reading this book who have a family member or close friend with bipolar disorder may become concerned that they, too, will face situations like those that follow. Put your mind at ease. I assure you Scotty's illness was much more severe than most. When manic, Scotty never realized he was sick and thus couldn't make rational decisions regarding treatment. For him, the illness erased anything resembling reality.

I have friends who are bipolar whose illness is less severe; for the most part, they manage their illness and live normal lives. Many have very successful careers, happy marriages, and children. They take their medications and are proactive, not reactive, to warning signs. Yes, they have a very serious mental illness, but they manage their illness — the illness does not manage them. These people are true role models for others struggling with this illness and are to be commended.

The chronicle of Scotty's mind on the run looks at the other side of the problem, where the person with bipolar is not able to care for himself. It is a look at what can and, more often, cannot be done by the family of the person who has bipolar disorder.

How can I recall so many details so completely? I once worked as the office manager for a large law firm in Washington, DC. The position required me to keep copious records, a practice that became ingrained. Throughout Scotty's illness, I kept a journal of his psychotic, manic behavior. In the midst of all the horror, optimism, disappointment, and struggle, a simple goal guided my journal: the hope that my notes might help his doctors better understand and treat his illness.

What follows is a straightforward account of heartbreaking disintegration, the unraveling of Scotty's life. It describes the impact on his wives and family, who all tried so hard to advocate for him. Additionally, it documents the gross inadequacies of a mental health system that failed to protect a man who could not protect himself.

Scotty, so full of talent, so determined to make a difference in the world, became a man beset by imagined threats and loneliness, with little control over his life. Witnessing this firsthand was a painful, frustrating experience. It was especially exasperating since the system designed to save him failed all of us so miserably.

No one in our family understood the magnitude of bipolar disorder in the beginning. The doctors told us after that first frightening episode that Scotty would be okay as long as he took his medication. We wanted to believe that. It restored our comfort level. None of us foresaw the nightmare that lay ahead.

Although painfully aware of the suicide statistics for sufferers of bipolar disorder, I held hope that Scotty would not follow that path. I hoped in vain. Scotty's sad journey ended in suicide on February 5, 2007. Some 32 years after first meeting this little eight-year-old boy standing next to his mother's casket, I returned to the same funeral home to say farewell. This cute little boy who had become such an important part of my life, this little boy I had mothered to adulthood, was no more. Across the years, his words from that first meeting came back to me.

"You know, my mother loved flowers. I sure wish she could see all the pretty flowers that people brought her."

He came into my life through tragedy — he left the same way.

2. WIRED AND OUT OF CONTROL

The Baker family was enjoying a good life. Toby was our anchor. Strong and wise. Generous. Some Christmases rather than buying gifts for one another, he'd give to the homeless. That was Toby. Give to someone else before himself.

Toby fell to cancer and though he fought bravely, a four-year battle took him from us in June 1992. Saddened by his father's death, Scotty gave no indication of having more than normal difficulty dealing with it. In fact, I admired his ability to quickly return to his demanding job and resume an active social life. A new girlfriend soon appeared on the scene and talk of marriage surfaced.

A few months later, they were engaged. Concerned that they hadn't known each other long enough, I tried to talk Scotty into a longer engagement. "Mom," he would say every time we had this somewhat confrontational discussion, "this is the wife of my dreams. I appreciate your concern, but trust me. I know what I'm doing here."

They married in August 1993, though they had dated less than a year, and made their home in nearby Centreville. All seemed well, but it was not — out-and-out disaster was coming.

Disasters fall into three camps. There are those you see coming from afar, a hurricane for instance or a raging forest fire. You have time to prepare and escape. Other disasters like tornadoes strike with little warning and quickly inflict lethal damage, but there's still a chance to take cover. Disasters of the third camp strike without warning and destroy everything. Moreover there's no way out. An earthquake brings your world tumbling down. It spares nothing.

On a Sunday morning in mid-December 1993, an early morning phone call awakened me. The call came from Scotty's youngest sister, Jodie, who lived in Fort Myers, Florida, with her husband, Alan. The early hour and tearful voice signaled a problem. A powerful, telling quake had struck Scotty the night before and the aftershocks and tremors would never abate.

"Mom, sorry to call so early," she said. "You're not going to believe what I'm about to tell you. We saw Scotty yesterday. He was in Fort Lauderdale on business. Something is wrong with him. He was completely out of control, almost like he's wired!"

"Jodie, what are you talking about?" I asked, half asleep.

"Scotty was like a maniac last night, high-strung and just downright obnoxious. He never stopped talking and made no sense at all.

"Mom, he drove us to dinner like a madman," she continued, "doing over 100! I've never seen him like that before. Alan and I were scared, but Scotty was acting so weird, we were afraid to say anything."

"Come on, Jodie," I said, "you're exaggerating."

"I'm not exaggerating, Mom," she said, shouting to make her point.

"Jodie, please calm down. Maybe he just had too much to drink."

"Mom, you don't understand. Scotty was not drunk! When we first walked into his hotel lobby, we heard him before we saw him. He was causing such a ruckus in the gift shop, the manager told him to leave or he would call the police! Scotty saw us, gave me a hug, and took us up to his room. He wasn't even embarrassed that he had just been kicked out of the store!"

"You won't believe his room. It was trashed, almost like a tornado hit it. Stuff was everywhere. He wrote all over a wall mirror with a magic marker, something motivational, maybe a Bible verse, I don't know. I didn't want to ask him. He never sat still. He paced back and forth, mumbling stuff that made no sense.

"Sarah won't even talk to him. Can you believe that? Scotty called her several times from the room. She hung up on him every time. Have you talked to her? Does she know what's wrong with him?"

"Jodie, I'm shocked. I don't know what to say. I'm sure everything will be okay. Don't worry," I assured her.

"Mom, you had to have been there. This is serious. He's a different person. I'm worried — just having dinner with him was unbelievable. He talked loud, people stared at him. I had to tell him to lower his voice several times. He just ignored me, almost as if he was on another planet and never heard me."

"He's starting a new company called 'Save the Animals.' He knows I love animals and wants me to run it.

"Wait till you hear this!" she exclaimed. "He has one million dollars in cash to invest in the company. He really thinks it will gross millions. He'll donate the money to benefit homeless animals.

"Mom, it gets worse. He's running political programs for Bill and Hillary Clinton! It's confidential. He told me not to tell anyone. He wants me to take charge of those, as well. I didn't know how to respond to him. I just sat there dumbfounded! What do you think is wrong with him?"

"I have no idea, Jodie," I told her. "I'm stunned by what you're telling me."

"We couldn't wait to leave the restaurant," she said, "but the drive back to the hotel made us wish we were still in the restaurant. I just knew we would crash.

"But this time," Jodie said, "Alan was irritated with Scotty's reckless driving and told him to slow down. Mom, he paid no attention to Alan, like he never heard him!"

Jodie described their return to the hotel, how Scotty insisted they go to the gift shop, where he wanted to buy them everything in the store. Once again, his manic behavior got him evicted. Twice in one evening, Scotty was told to leave the premises. Showing no signs of embarrassment, rather joking about it, he insisted they return to his room and call Sarah. Jodie declined. They said goodbye in the lobby and drove back to Fort Myers, a good three-hour drive.

Jodie's phone call upset me. I was flabbergasted by her description of Scotty's behavior and did my best to console her and assure her it was probably alcohol related.

"Mom, it wasn't alcohol related," she quickly responded. "I'm telling you something is seriously wrong."

"You're probably right, Jodie, but let's keep this conversation between the two of us until I can talk with other family members." She agreed to do so.

At times like this, I missed Toby. He would know what to do. I didn't. Knowing Scotty drank too much alcohol, I'd discussed my concerns with him many times. His drug use in high school had also been a concern. I felt his behavior was either alcohol or drug related, perhaps a combination of both, and I would ask his older brother, Buddy, for advice. At least, I thought I would.

Procrastination set in. I didn't want to burden Buddy. He shared my concerns about his brother's drinking, and I didn't want to worry him. Uncertain how to confront Scotty on his weird behavior without involving Jodie, I took the easy way out. I did nothing. I buried my head in the sand and reassured myself it was just a one-time, bizarre incident that would never happen again.

But the fault deep within Scotty was active. An earthquake struck again. Early in January 1994, Sarah began calling Scotty's sister, Tricia, who lived in Norfolk, Virginia.

"I'm really worried about Scotty," she told Tricia. "He's acting weird! He doesn't sleep. He has become extremely religious and talks constantly about God's plans for him."

By mid-January, he was involuntarily hospitalized. It was clear that something was very wrong with Scotty. None of us had ever witnessed such psychotic behavior. To make matters worse, we possessed a limited collective knowledge of mental illness.

On January 18, 1994, Scotty spent his 27th birthday in a padded cell in the psychiatric ward at Inova Fairfax Hospital in Falls Church, Virginia. His family could view him on camera only. Inova diagnosed Scotty as having bipolar disorder and transferred him to the Woodburn Center for Community Mental Health in nearby Annandale.

"This place is not really a hospital," Scotty told us. "It's a training ground for the CIA. My room is bugged. All my conversations are monitored. These people are not doctors and nurses. They're actors."

Notorious for playing practical jokes on people, he was not joking now. He was serious, and he believed what he was saying. We were dumbfounded.

One evening during Scotty's confinement at Woodburn, I took Sarah to dinner to alleviate her fears about Scotty's mental condition and reassure her he would get well. After dinner, we stopped by Woodburn to visit Scotty. As we entered the hospital, Sarah's father was just leaving.

"Come back home, Sarah," he said, shaking his head from side to side. "This situation is hopeless."

Sarah and I went to Scotty's room. Along the way, we encountered many mentally ill patients. Their conditions were severe, and the overall effect was upsetting and frightening to Sarah. I was frightened, too, but hid my fears. Some of these poor people were just sitting or standing in the hallway with a blank stare. Others were carrying on conversations with people apparently only they could see. The patients who really scared Sarah were the ones who followed us, ranting and raving incoherently. Scotty at least recognized us, knew his name and where he was, and could talk.

After giving us a hug, Scotty placed his forefinger to his lips, leaned toward us, and whispered, "I'm unable to speak freely. Everything I say is being recorded by the Secret Service. This place is full of agents, some of them good guys, others not so good, so be careful what you say," he cautioned us.

Completely losing her composure at this point, Sarah ran out of the hospital crying.

"What the heck is wrong with her?" Scotty asked.

"Oh, she's just upset because you're in the hospital" I assured him. "I'll go check on her and come back another time."

Our visit was brief. Following Sarah to the car, I struggled to maintain my composure. I drove her home and pulled into a nearby shopping center, where I had my own private meltdown.

Throughout his stay at Woodburn, Scotty called frequently to share his psychotic thoughts. Unfortunately, most calls came during the night with no regard for the hour. It never occurred to him that I had to get to the office early the next morning and might be sleeping. I repeatedly asked him to call during the day, and he always agreed to do so. Nevertheless, the late night calls continued. He was awake with his racing, delusional thoughts and assumed everybody else was awake, too.

During one such call, he lowered his voice to a whisper and asked, "Can you keep a secret?"

"Yes," I assured him.

"I'm in the Witness Protection Program," he continued in a whispered tone. "You must keep this confidential, Mom. It's not clear whom I can trust. This place is not only full of Secret Service agents, but the FBI also has a strong presence."

Another late night call came from a fellow patient at Woodburn.

"This is the White House calling," he said. "Please remain on the line for an important call from the President."

Scotty got on the line and proudly announced, "Mom, you're talking to the president of the United States. Can you believe your son is the president? Now listen to me carefully," he said. "I'm in the middle of a very important cabinet meeting. We're hungry. I need you to deliver enough pizzas to feed us. We're working hard to solve the problems in this country."

I always agreed to purchase and deliver pizza to appease Scotty. He was always so serious. Other family members received these same pizza delivery requests. By this time, we were all beyond being dumbfounded. He was so ill. The prospect that he might never recover haunted us all.

But recover he did after a month of treatment. Initial progress was slow, but after the first ten days of treatment with forced medications, we began to see encouraging signs of improvement. The Woodburn staff was wonderful. Scotty received extensive counseling on how to cope with and manage bipolar disorder and recognize signs of recurrence. His wonderful doctor continued with outpatient treatment and remained Scotty's longtime psychiatrist.

Our elation about his recovery and release, however, was soon diminished. Sarah moved back home with her parents. She subsequently filed for divorce after only ten months of marriage. They had no children. Her parents could not cope with the stigma of a mentally ill son-in-law and had encouraged Sarah to file for divorce.

Scotty continued to live in the Centreville house he'd shared with Sarah during their short marriage. Devastated by her abrupt departure and their subsequent divorce, he still made a concerted effort to pick up the pieces and move on. He saw his doctor regularly and took his medication.

The drug prescribed to treat Scotty's bipolar disorder was lithium. NAMI defines it as "a drug used in the treatment of acute mania and as a maintenance medication to help reduce the duration, intensity, and frequency of manic episodes. There is, however, a narrow margin in the effectiveness of this drug. Toxicity occurs with too high a dosage, and too low a dosage results in no effect in the treatment of this illness. Because it is important to maintain the therapeutic level of lithium in the blood within a certain range, lithium levels must be monitored with blood tests."

We all tried to remain optimistic that Scotty's awful illness was a one-time occurrence, and that lithium would prevent it from happening again. We were so wrong.

The so-called "one-time occurrence" marked the beginning of our family's nightmare. Scotty was wired and out of control. The deadly earthquake that had struck without warning continued to shake our world apart and even worse, more quakes, aftershocks, and tremors were on the way.

3. GOOD TIMES, BAD TIMES, SAD TIMES

Coping with the stigma of mental illness and the loss of Sarah, Scotty struggled throughout the rest of 1994. It was a difficult time for him and the family. We witnessed his struggle firsthand. Once considered the life of every party (even if there was no party), Scotty looked like a man shouldering the weight of the world.

Scotty and I got together frequently. I was widowed. He was divorced. We kept each other company. We discussed his illness. At times, embarrassed about it, Scotty wanted to put it behind him and pretend it never happened. Other times, he wanted to talk. "Why me?" was a question that lived inside him.

"We'll never know the answer to that question," I said. "Apparently you inherited this gene. Your mother suffered from severe depression. Although never diagnosed with bipolar disorder, perhaps her condition was never correctly diagnosed."

I told him that some people with this gene develop bipolar disorder, while others do not. "You developed bipolar, while your three siblings, thus far, have been spared. I've read that stressful events such as the death of a loved one may trigger the first episode. Perhaps in your case, it was the death of your Dad, maybe adjusting to marriage, both of which were major changes in your life. We'll just never know."

I asked him not to dwell on the "why me?" but, instead, focus on managing the misfortune he'd been dealt. "You're a very strong person Scotty," I assured him over and over. "If anybody can deal with bipolar disorder, it's you."

We had many heart-to-heart talks. Each time I reminded him that his father, for whom he had the utmost respect, would tell him the same thing were he alive.

After one such heart-to-heart talk, I received an oversized delivery of gorgeous fresh flowers at my office. The card read: "You're successful, smart, loving, good-humored, and pretty. I've always loved you, but guess I had to grow up to realize how much I admire you, too." It was signed, "With love from your son, Scott," followed by his customary "happy face" drawing.

I was touched that day by his thoughtfulness. He always had such a nice way with words, and over the years, I accumulated quite a stash of Scotty cards and notes.

One of his New Year's resolutions at the beginning of 1995 was to "get over it," as he put it, and that he did. That year was a happy one for all of us as we enjoyed the return of the warm, gentle, kindhearted Scotty with his unique outgoing personality and sense of humor. It was great to have him back, and I was so proud of him.

By early 1996, Scotty was not only enjoying a very active social life again, but was also doing well in his professional CPA life. Life was good.

This "good life," however, was short lived. Several months later, yet another problem plagued Scotty. Concerns about the side effects of lithium took center stage. Like most medications, lithium produces its share of side effects, and, for some, the drug is not tolerable. Scotty's cross to bear included weight gain and hand tremors, and he was concerned about the possible damage lithium could do to his kidneys.

Many people can't deal with lithium's side effects and stop taking it. We feared Scotty would do the same.

"Just look at me! I look like a fat slob! I hate looking like this."

"Scotty," I told him every time this subject came up, "the weight gain and hand tremors, although difficult to cope with, are a small price to pay to control your illness. I wish you didn't have to deal with them, but you must."

"Easy for you to say," he said. "How would you feel about a 20-pound weight gain and shaking hands?"

My response was always the same. "I'd prefer them to mania."

Scotty was right. It was easy for me to say. I hated that he had to deal with the horrible side effects of a medication he'd have to take for the rest of his life, but not taking lithium was not an option. I found I had to be very careful with my lectures, always striving to show compassion, but at the same time remaining firm.

For me, good things began to happen. In September 1996, I remarried and my husband, George Pacharis, and I made our home in Fairfax, Virginia. We first met in a bereavement group, our spouses having died around the same time following lengthy illnesses. He knew about my son's illness and was not only supportive and sympathetic, but enjoyed Scotty's outgoing personality and spending time with him. We all got together as often as we possibly could.

Good things began to happen in Scotty's life as well. He had a new girlfriend. I hadn't seen him this happy in a long time. I was so grateful. For two years, the bipolar nightmare began to fade. Life approached normality and good things happened, things like sports and outdoor recreation.

Scotty loved football. Growing up in the metropolitan Washington, DC, area, he ardently followed the Washington Redskins. Through a business connection, he picked up tickets for the 1996 season. Glory days! For Scotty, it was never important if the team won or lost. The magic of just being there took center stage. The 1996 season was the Redskins' last season to play at RFK Stadium, and, to Scotty, being there meant being a part of history itself.

Looking for something to do one Saturday afternoon after football season ended, Scotty attended a boat show with a friend. On a whim, he purchased an 18-foot Magnum speedboat. Classic Scotty. He had no plans to buy a boat; it just struck his fancy as a good idea at the time. Throughout the summer, every weekend became a boating weekend. He loved the water, the outdoors, and the exhilaration of driving the boat at top speed, and he learned a few things along the way, too.

A bit sheepish, he confided in us about the first time he trailered the boat to nearby Lake Anna. He had neglected to secure the boat cushions and watched in horror as they sailed out of the boat on Interstate 95. Fortunately, he pulled over on the shoulder and gathered them without incident.

In early 1998, Scotty began to show signs of restlessness, discontent, and boredom. After eight years as a public accountant, he complained that the profession had grown monotonous. It was no longer challenging. It was time for him to move on.

He had dreamed of owning his own company since childhood, and his dream became a reality in the winter of 1998. He started a company, Prosperity Technical Services Inc. (PTSI), a search firm recruiting information technology people for technical positions in the DC metropolitan area. Starting with one employee, he worked out of a small office in Merrifield, Virginia.

Scotty liked being his own boss. His outgoing personality and love of sales that had served him so well during his bike shop days continued to be a great asset. Working long days, weekends, and holidays, Scotty soon became an entrepreneurial success. He never met a stranger and thrived on cold call sales, something most people shy away from. PTSI became so successful within the first year that it was necessary to hire additional employees. With this increase in staff, the company outgrew its space in Merrifield, and Scotty moved the office to a larger location in nearby Fairfax.

Even with his workaholic schedule, Scotty made time for his new love. On December 11, 1999, surprising us all, he became engaged to Sarah Jordan, whom he had dated for four and a half years. It was a mere coincidence that his first wife and soon-to-be new wife shared the same first name.

The new Sarah and Scotty met in March 1995 at a restaurant in Springfield. Sarah was there with friends, as was Scotty. She was completing an internship for her final three credits at Virginia Tech and working part-time as a waitress.

Their engagement was unique. On a White House tour, while in the Blue Room, Scotty persuaded the Secret Service agents to let him and Sarah stand inside the roped-off area next to the Christmas tree and fireplace. On his knees, he proposed and gave Sarah a beautiful, expensive engagement ring. The Secret Service and 50 or so other people in the tour group looked on and applauded.

By this time, George and I had retired. We lived in Florida during the winter and in Maryland during the summer months.

When Scotty called me in Florida to tell me the news, he volunteered that he'd gotten the idea for a "White House Engagement" during one of his recent White House tours. He thought it was unique, a story he would some day tell his grandchildren.

"June 17, 2000. Save the date for the wedding of the century," he told me.

Recalling his obsession with the White House and president during his previous breakdown, it troubled me that he was taking White House tours and had chosen this location to propose to Sarah. I could have dismissed these concerns as over-reaction on my part had I not received an alarming letter from Scotty the following day.

This three-page letter, handwritten by Scotty on stationary from the Phoenix Hotel in Washington, DC, summarized his religious thoughts on a portion of the Ten Commandments and unjust slavery in this country. He quoted Bible verses from the New Testament and listed several prayers he suggested I say daily.

Reading his letter, I cringed. Still, I managed to convince myself that this somewhat neurotic religious frenzy was a false alarm. It was not.

My concerns about the White House also proved valid. Our excitement about the upcoming wedding died. This time, we knew what was happening. Scotty was sick again. His hypomanic phase quickly intensified into full-blown mania in January 2000, six years after his first episode.

4. Please, Not Again

"Oh, please, may this not be happening again," I thought. But I knew it was.

We all knew.

Removing his shirt at the office, walking around bare-chested, spreading toilet tissue all over the yard, and egging the house where Sarah lived with roommates. Dumping several hundred dollars' worth of coins all over his church parking lot and writing a $10,000 check to his church — all of these were telltale signs of mania.

"Use the $10,000 check to develop a youth center," he told his minister.

Generous charitable contributions were not unusual for Scotty. He was generous. His philosophy on charitable giving was "give till it hurts. Then, give just a little bit more." But a $10,000 check to develop a youth center... definitely not the norm.

Scotty, aware that his family was worried, drove himself to the Woodburn Center for Community Mental Health to convince us he was not manic, a futile attempt. He left before the staff could evaluate him. Scotty knew the doctor would recommend he admit himself for treatment. He was in denial and not about to admit himself.

Scotty, being an adult, had to give his consent for us to admit him for treatment. Without his consent, we were helpless to help him. Virginia law is explicit, very specific. The law requires that someone

23

with a severe mental illness must be an "imminent danger to self or others" before that person can be involuntarily committed for treatment. This legal provision would come back to haunt us all.

Scotty had not yet fallen into the "imminent danger" category, and in the interim, we were helpless. We had no choice but to sit and watch him deteriorate mentally until he became suicidal or homicidal. Only then could we arrange a hearing and have him involuntarily treated.

And sit by helplessly we did as Scotty unraveled.

"I'm purchasing 45 acres in Berryville, Virginia," he announced out of the blue one day. "I'll donate this land to the United Methodist Church, named in honor of Jesus Christ, my personal cure for manic depression. A manic episode is a wake-up call from God. I'm not crazy, God is leading me. I'm manic for God! I've purchased 100,000 Bibles," he told us. "Every young person who logs onto my new website at church gets a free Bible."

Still trying to convince his family he was okay, perhaps himself as well, he let his brother, Buddy, drive him to Georgetown University Hospital in Washington, DC, for evaluation. Again though, he left the hospital before the staff could evaluate him, knowing full well the doctor would urge him to admit himself.

Full-blown manic but in complete denial, Scotty insisted that he and Sarah proceed with their dinner plans that evening to celebrate her mother's birthday at a local restaurant.

"Meet me at the restaurant with your parents," he instructed Sarah.

Concerned about Scotty's manic condition, his brother, Chris, who lived in Centreville near Scotty, accompanied Sarah to the restaurant. They found him lying on the sidewalk outside the restaurant, smoking a cigar on an extremely cold winter night in January. He was dressed in a business suit with no topcoat.

"Scotty," Chris yelled, "what the heck are you doing?"

"What does it look like I'm doing?" he responded, calm and cool. "I'm enjoying a smoke and relaxing on the sidewalk."

"Sarah," Chris whispered, "I think you should go in alone and have dinner with your parents. They shouldn't see Scotty in this condition. I'll keep him occupied out here."

Sarah went in alone. Over dinner, she told her parents — they had arrived before Scotty was lying on the sidewalk — that Scotty was bipolar and having a manic episode. Neither parent was familiar with bipolar disorder or manic episodes, nor had Sarah ever witnessed a manic episode, and she did her best to downplay Scotty's condition, not wanting to worry her parents about their future son-in-law's mental stability.

After dinner, Sarah took Scotty home with her. She shared a townhouse with two roommates. The four spent the night talking, but all was not well.

Chris received an alarming phone call from Sarah early the next morning.

"Chris! Scotty never went to sleep last night. He was up all night. I hid his car keys so he couldn't drive. He got mad and left on foot. It's 29 degrees outside, and he's walking to the office with no coat. I don't know what to do!"

"I'll see if I can track him down, Sarah," he told her. "Try not to worry. I'll call you when I find him."

En route to his office, Scotty encountered a homeless man on the street. Without hesitation, he offered the man a job at his company. He gave the man his personal Visa credit card.

"Go get something to eat and buy yourself some new clothes before you report for work," he told him.

Scotty, with his big heart, was always generous to those less fortunate. He often purchased food for them and gave them cash, but he had never given strangers his Visa card. It was something the normal Scotty would never do.

A brisk, two-hour walk later, Scotty telephoned Sarah from his office. Somehow, she convinced him to go to the hospital. Chris picked him up and drove him to Sibley Hospital in Washington, DC, but once again, Scotty left before the staff could evaluate him and took a taxi back to his office.

Joe, one of Scotty's first employees at PTSI and a good friend, was also concerned about his boss's psychotic condition. He persuaded Scotty to return to Sibley Hospital. This time — to our surprise and relief — Scotty voluntarily admitted himself.

Joe, though unaware his boss was bipolar, recognized his recent behavior was not normal. Scotty was spending a lot of time at the bike shop across the street and less time in the office.

"I'm thinking about buying that shop," he confided to Joe. "It brings back memories of my high school bike shop days."

Religion had also become a big part of Scotty's life, and he spoke often of entering the seminary. Joe drove Scotty to a seminary in Washington, DC, for enrollment purposes. The staff quickly recognized that Scotty was ill and took extra time to visit with him.

Joe knew about the federal agents and Scotty's many trips to the White House. He knew about Scotty's $10,000 contribution to the Ronald McDonald House on behalf of Hillary Clinton. This contribution more or less confirmed Joe's suspicions that his boss was not well, especially since Scotty had never spoken highly of Mrs. Clinton.

— ▪ —

As Scotty settled into hospital life at Sibley, boredom and discontent became his roommates in short order. He began burning up the phone lines to family and friends. My first call came on January 13. He jumped from one subject to another, as he always did when manic. I just listened.

"Mom, I'm a patient at Sibley Hospital," he announced with pride. "You know, the miracle hospital. I've been trying to get into this place for a long time. Well, here I am. Don't tell anyone, but God has commissioned me to write another chapter for the Bible. Can you believe that after 2000 years, he selected me for this important project? I get goose bumps just thinking about the privilege he has bestowed upon me."

"Talked with your old law firm today," he said, abruptly changing the subject. "I'm filing enough class action lawsuits to keep them busy for the next 20 years."

"Don't tell Sarah this, but I can't marry her. I'm a Prophet of God and not allowed to marry," switching from class action lawsuits to being a Prophet of God.

Convinced, as he was beyond any doubt, that God had anointed him a prophet, I still felt the need to respond, "Scotty, you're manic again. You're very, very sick. Please believe me when I tell you that you're not a Prophet of God. I'm so glad you're at Sibley and getting the treatment you need to get well."

Soon after this conversation, Scotty attempted to leave the hospital and for some reason became very violent. The hospital staff, amazed by his strength and resistance, was forced to restrain and sedate him.

Even more determined to leave the next day, he packed his bag, wrote a note to the hospital administrator, delivered the note to the nurses' station, and requested that it be placed in his file.

The note said, "I, Scott Baker, am being held against my will."

The nurse on duty accepted the note.

"Return to your room," she instructed him, "or go to solitary confinement."

Returning to his room was not part of his plan that day. Instead, he made another attempt to leave, and this time the staff called security for backup. During the scuffle, Scotty hit one of the security guards, was placed in a four-point restraint, and was removed to solitary confinement.

Because he had assaulted the guard, he now fell into the category of "imminent danger to others." His doctor requested a meeting with family members to discuss treatment options. Buddy met with the doctor, who proposed three options:

1) Scotty could agree to take his medications and be treated at Sibley.
2) The doctor could have him committed to another hospital.
3) Scotty's family could have him committed to another facility.

Buddy requested that the doctor continue treatment at Sibley.

The following day, Scotty's older sisters, Kathy and Tricia, who lived in the Norfolk, Virginia, area, drove from their homes to visit him. Upon entering the psychiatric ward, they saw Scotty at the nurses' station, where he was yelling at the nurse demanding she contact his doctor. He saw his sisters and said "hi" as though they were hospital workers, not his sisters who had just driven four hours to visit him.

Having been placed in a four-point restraint the previous night, he was still furious.

"This frickin' place wouldn't even let me up to use the bathroom. I had to pee in my bed," he complained to his sisters.

Humiliated, he was determined to leave.

Pacing back and forth to the nurses' station, Scotty yelled, "Either contact my doctor or let me out of this place!"

Pacing furiously, he saw the locked security door of the psychiatric ward open to let someone enter. As his sisters looked on in disbelief, he seized the moment and darted out the door, hit the elevator, and bolted.

Neither sister could believe what Scotty had just done. They had actually witnessed their brother's escape. They dashed down seven flights of stairs to the street. He was nowhere to be seen, not in the lobby, nor on the street. Rushing back to the seventh floor, they expected the staff to help them in the search for their mentally ill brother. To their dismay, the hospital staff simply expressed regret.

"Sorry, it's unfortunate, it happens sometimes. We have other patients, our staff is limited, and we can't help you search for your brother."

Scotty resurfaced at his office later in the day wearing a woman's wig. He bragged to anyone who would listen about his escape from Sibley Hospital.

His next stop was Sarah's house. Her roommates, having recently spent time with Scotty, knew only too well that he was very ill, and although they cared deeply for him, his presence made them uncomfortable. As a courtesy to them, Sarah asked Scotty to leave.

Not the least bit offended, Scotty left. Dressed in a business suit, with his Bible in hand, he headed for the White House.

"I'm Scott Baker," he informed the Secret Service. "I'm here for a very important meeting with President Clinton. I have information he needs to solve the poverty problems in this country."

"The president is not available to meet with you," the agent responded and instructed Scotty to leave the White House grounds. Fortunately, he did not press the issue and complied with the agent's instructions.

Back in his car, he returned to Sibley Hospital, where he saw a police officer directing traffic. Scotty convinced the officer to go with him to the psychiatric ward, where he demanded the arrest of the entire staff. The officer tried to get Scotty to commit himself but was unsuccessful.

Scotty returned to his car, where in his bipolar world, he saw the black van that had been following him since he left the White House. He was convinced the van was following him because he was to become the next president of the United States with Hillary Clinton as his vice president. The van followed him to his office, parked outside his building, and waited for him while he worked well into the night — in his mind, at least.

Around midnight, he emailed me.

"Working hard, Mom," he said. "Just set up 40 new companies. I feel better than I've ever felt in my life," his email continued. "Mania is simply the Holy Spirit. Get your Bible out and read the Book of Job, chapters nine through 16. You'll see what I mean. While you're at it, read the Book of Ecclesiastes, chapter five, to learn about Abraham and Sarah."

Emails like this one always upset me. I was angry and frustrated because we could do nothing to help him. Instead, with each passing day — because of the law — we were forced to watch him slip farther away.

Taking matters into his own hands, Buddy contacted the Fairfax County police.

"My brother is bipolar, off his meds, and dangerous," he told them.

The police agreed to meet Buddy at the health spa where Scotty was getting a weekly massage for a chronic back problem. The police would transport Scotty to Mount Vernon Hospital in Alexandria, Virginia, where he'd be held for 72 hours while Buddy arranged a hearing to, hopefully, have Scotty involuntarily committed for treatment.

When the police arrived at the spa, it was as if Scotty expected them. He proudly showed them a law book and recited his rights.

"I acknowledge I'm bipolar," he told the police. "I see my doctor regularly, and I take my medications. It's not illegal to be mentally ill. You can't take me into custody unless I'm suicidal or homicidal. I'm neither," he declared.

Scotty had done his homework and knew his rights.

The next day, accompanied by his pastor, Scotty checked himself into Georgetown University Hospital in Washington, DC. He left a message on Sarah's answering machine.

"I realize I'm ill," his message said. "I'm at Georgetown Hospital getting help."

"What a relief," I thought, although my relief was short-lived.

The following day, Scotty executed his second escape from a mental hospital in less than a week. The staff, surprised that any patient could escape unnoticed from such an exceptionally secure facility, expressed regret.

"This is the second hospital to express regret," I thought. I was outraged! How could Sibley and Georgetown Hospitals let a mentally ill person escape? Scotty had outsmarted the very people charged with the responsibility of caring for him.

The doctor on staff subsequently informed us that Scotty had slept only two hours the previous night. He'd refused all medications and had become emotional when talking about the approaching 25th anniversary of his mother's death.

Considering Scotty's earlier escape the same week, you'd have thought the staff would have been more watchful and used more precautionary measures. But no, they merely "expressed regret." We'd been down the "road of regret," and it no longer worked for us. We were angry, to say the least, and handcuffed by mental health laws and regulations.

We had our own regrets about the torture that Scotty's mind on the run was putting him through, and the hospital's hollow apology provided no solace. We regretted that the law could backfire so horribly, endangering our loved one. It was maddening for us all. An old proverb holds that well-fed horses don't rampage. We were starving horses rampaging for some real way to help Scotty. Some way that would put "Please, Not Again" away for good.

5. A Law Gone Awry

Several days went by with no word from Scotty. We feared the worst. All of us. Then, as if nothing out of the ordinary had happened, Sarah received a call.

"I've joined the Army and Navy Club and will be here for a few days," Scotty told her.

The Army and Navy Club, a prestigious, private, for-members-only club in downtown Washington, DC, consists of active and retired military personnel from all branches of the Armed Forces, as well as civilian personnel in the Armed Forces. It includes presidents, vice presidents, members of Congress, and cabinet officials. It takes at least four weeks for the membership committee to process new applications, yet somehow Scotty, in his manic condition, had obtained overnight accommodations at this private club.

Throughout the night, Scotty left a stream of phone messages for his psychiatrist, the same doctor who had treated him since his first manic episode.

"I'm not sick," Scotty told him. "You're trying to poison me with those pills."

"Okay, I'll take the medicine," he said in a subsequent message. But ten minutes later, "No way are you going to poison me! Why should I take pills? I'm not sick. I don't need medicine," he yelled, slamming down the phone.

His sister, Kathy, received his next call, a string of rambling declarations.

"I've purchased a $5,000 electric guitar with an amplifier system. Don't know how to play, but I'll learn. The president asked my advice on how to solve the poverty problems in this country. I just mailed him a letter.

"I visited our mother's grave today and made arrangements to have it dug up for DNA testing," he said matter-of-factly. "Arlington National Cemetery has agreed to move her body from the cemetery in Fairfax to Dad's grave at Arlington. They should be together in death. Our mother was a saint, Kathy. Do you know that? Because of her, a cure for mental illness has been found in God."

Scotty's psychiatrist was kind enough to call in a prescription for an antipsychotic drug. He said it would work quickly *if* Scotty agreed to take it. Sarah picked up the prescription and delivered it to Scotty at the club. He refused to take it. Realizing she could do nothing more, she left. On her way out, she spoke privately with the manager on duty and explained Scotty's situation.

With no reason to assume I could be any more successful than Sarah in persuading him to take the drug, I called Scotty. Quickly recognizing my voice, he began yelling.

"Don't ask me how I'm doing. I'm fine. I don't need your advice. I'm very busy right now making arrangements for a nice romantic dinner with my fiancée. What do you want?" he asked in a very angry and disrespectful voice.

I knew from Scotty's tone that I had to choose my words carefully and proceed with caution. "Scotty," I said, "your family is very worried about you. You're manic again. The only way to get well is to take your medicine."

He literally exploded.

"Take care of yourself and leave me alone. Don't you ever call me again," he screamed. "I've been manic all my life. How can you not know that? I'm tired of people telling me to take my medicine."

Our conversation went downhill quickly. I persisted. "Scotty, you're too sick right now to know you're sick. Please trust your family on this one," I pleaded, "and take the medicine Sarah brought you."

"Trust you?" he screamed. "You're all trying to poison me. Go get a life, Mom, and get the fuck out of mine!"

Scotty beat me to it and slammed down the phone. Our heated conversation was brief, and I felt I had only worsened a difficult situation. I started crying, and once again spent a sleepless "Scotty night."

Sarah didn't return to the club to join Scotty for dinner. They, too, had words on the phone about bipolar disorder and taking his medicine. When she called later to check on him, he had gone. Sarah felt certain that Scotty was forced to leave because of his disruptive behavior.

After many unsuccessful attempts, Kathy finally reached Scotty on his cell phone. He was on his way to the Blackstone Retreat in Blackstone, Virginia, a three-hour drive from Washington, DC.

"I'll have my own fucking retreat," he yelled. In a manic rage, he repeatedly used the F word to describe Sarah and me. "I threw my medicine out the window a few miles back, and I'm filing attempted murder charges against my psychiatrist for trying to kill me with drugs," he shouted.

Concerned about what her brother might do at the Blackstone Retreat, Kathy alerted the manager that her mentally ill brother was headed their way. She explained the severity of his illness.

"I'm sorry you have to deal with this. Don't hesitate to call the police if my brother gets out of control or refuses to leave the premises," she told the manager, "and then please call me."

As expected, Scotty's manic behavior alarmed the staff at Blackstone, leaving the manager with no choice but to call the police. Once again, he recited his rights.

"I'm bipolar, I take my medicine, I'm not suicidal or homicidal," he assured the police officers.

When confronted by law enforcement, Scotty possessed an uncanny ability to keep his mania intact long enough to convince them he was not a danger to himself or others. He knew the magic words that worked with each police encounter — "I'm not suicidal or homicidal," and once again, he was allowed to drive away.

His sister, Tricia, received the next call. He was en route to Cary, North Carolina, to visit a childhood friend.

"I'm tossing my cell phone," he told her. "The Secret Service has it bugged and I can't use it anymore. I'm scared, Tricia, I'm really scared. I fear for my life," he said quite emotionally. "Federal agents are trying to kill me. What should I do?"

"Scotty, you're being paranoid. There's nothing to be afraid of," she assured him.

While on the way to Cary in Lawrenceville, Virginia, Scotty saw several state trooper cars pulled over near the North Carolina border along the side of the highway due to icy conditions. He pulled off the highway behind them.

"I'm very tired," he explained to the troopers. "Federal agents are after me. They're trying to kill me. What I'm about to tell you is very confidential," he whispered. "I'm in possession of top secret information that will embarrass the United States government if I go public. You have to help me," he pleaded.

"Take my car keys," he said, handing them over to the troopers. "Will you please drive me to my friend's house in Cary?" he begged.

The troopers, recognizing that Scotty was ill, drove him to the Brunswick County sheriff's office. Scotty gave them Sarah's telephone number, and a trooper told her of Scotty's location.

A bed was found for him at the Poplar Springs Hospital in nearby Petersburg, where he was transported and held for a hearing.

Scotty's regular psychiatrist gave the hospital Scotty's background information and medical history. He alerted the staff to Scotty's track record of escapes so that extra precautions could be taken.

Kathy called the hospital to get information on Scotty's condition, only to receive the hospital's standard response:

"Due to the Health Insurance Portability and Accountability Act of 1996 (HIPAA), this hospital is unable to release any information without the consent of the patient. Your brother refuses to give permission. I can tell you nothing," the nurse said, snippy and unsympathetic.

Letting Scotty exercise his right to privacy under HIPAA was more than foolhardy; it was a disservice to him and his family. Enforced by the blind eye of bureaucracy, HIPAA prevented the very people who cared about Scotty from getting the information needed to make intelligent decisions about his treatment. A manic Scotty could not — and should not — make those decisions. This backfiring legislation for Scotty morphed into a calamitous catch-22. It left him and his family headed for catastrophe. It was nothing short of a miscarriage of justice, medicine turned upside down.

The nurse's standard, self-righteous "HIPAA response" was typical. She could have shown a little compassion and responded to Kathy in a more comforting way. She didn't.

Despite the nurse's curt attitude, Kathy managed to find out the date of the hearing so she and Tricia could attend on the family's behalf. Without benefit of legal counsel, they prepared for the hearing and compiled a list of Scotty's psychotic actions of the last few weeks. Kathy read the list to the judge.

Courtesy of the State of Virginia taxpayers, patients at involuntary commitment hearings received free legal representation. Scotty declined this service, choosing to represent himself. When his time came to speak, he pleaded his case with the finesse of an accomplished trial lawyer, kept his cool, and was polite to the judge. Scotty's performance astounded Kathy and Tricia.

Two doctors on the hospital staff testified that Scotty should be involuntarily committed for treatment. Thankfully, the judge accepted their recommendations and ruled that Scotty would be committed for up to 30 days, stipulating he could be released any time his doctor felt that he was well enough to leave. The hospital placed Scotty in its most secure area.

Not the least bit angry with Kathy for her role in having him involuntarily committed, Scotty was certain that being committed was part of God's plan. However, the next day a bad snowstorm kept the local psychiatrist assigned to him from getting to the hospital. Scotty spent his day writing a complaint letter to the governor of Virginia, protesting his temporary detention order at Poplar Springs.

On day three, the doctor broke the distressing news that Scotty's insurance company would only approve a four-day stay in the hospital.

"I'm trying to get an extension to seven days," the doctor explained to Kathy.

"My brother is so psychotic right now," she said, "I don't think he will even be well enough to leave in a week. Can't you keep him longer?" she pleaded.

"I agree your brother is very ill, but you have to understand my position. I'm caught up in the bureaucracy of the insurance system. Insurance companies decide how long patients remain in the hospital, not doctors."

The doctor's admission shocked me. Where was his backbone in confronting the bureaucratic insurance companies and doing what was in his patient's best interest? He was a psychiatrist, trained to treat the mentally ill, with firsthand knowledge that these patients don't get well overnight.

"Furthermore," the doctor continued, "a contributing factor to your brother's continued psychotic behavior is that he's taking his medicine reluctantly."

"My brother is not only taking his meds reluctantly," she said with exasperation, "he's probably not taking them at all. He knows how to play the medicine game, pretending to swallow the pills but removing them from his mouth once the nurse leaves the room. He must be closely supervised with his meds; otherwise, they end up in the toilet. The staff has to do mouth checks," she insisted, "or my brother will never get well."

This information prompted the doctor to arrange a second hearing, wherein the judge ordered forced medications should Scotty refuse to take them. With this ruling, Kathy felt that Scotty finally understood he must take his medications or he wouldn't be released. He also seemed to understand that if his stay exceeded the seven days his insurance company had approved, he could be transferred to a Virginia state mental hospital.

During his stay at Poplar Springs, Sarah spoke with Scotty daily. One weekend, she drove from northern Virginia to tell him in person that she was postponing the wedding.

"I'm not canceling it, Scotty," she assured him. "I'm only postponing it until we can work out your bipolar situation."

Her words troubled Scotty, but he seemed to understand.

Soon thereafter, we received the unsettling news that Scotty would be discharged after nine days, with the understanding that he would immediately return to Fairfax for outpatient treatment with his regular doctor. We all knew Scotty wasn't well enough to leave and felt it was unlikely he'd return to Fairfax for outpatient treatment.

Tricia called Scotty's doctor to question his decision.

"Your brother, although not well, is in fair condition," he said.

Taking a taxi from the hospital to his car, Scotty wasted no time leaving the Petersburg area. Heading north on a rural road, he saw an

Interstate 95 sign. Two options faced him: take I-95 north and return to Fairfax, where he could continue outpatient treatment, or head south.

"I'm on my way to Fort Myers Beach, Florida, to visit Mom and George," he told Sarah.

A tearful call from Scotty awakened Tricia at 5:10 AM the following morning.

"I'm in a Florida hotel. I think I'm safe, at least for the moment. I can't stop shaking. I'm so scared, Trish. There are people outside the hotel waiting to kill me. White vans followed me all the way from Virginia."

Tricia did her best to assure Scotty he was safe. She then called his doctor at Poplar Springs. "My brother is in Florida, not Virginia."

"I'm sorry he made such a poor decision," was the good doctor's response.

How could this doctor expect Scotty to make anything but a "poor decision?" You don't release a severely mentally ill patient whose condition the doctor himself described as "not well, but in fair condition," and expect him to make good choices. Rather than confronting Scotty's insurance company, the wimpy doctor let insurance bureaucrats decide how long Scotty would remain hospitalized for treatment.

Later in the day, still fearing for his life, Scotty checked out of the hotel and continued south, where he sought refuge at his uncle's house in Brandon, Florida. His uncle had his prescriptions for lithium and an antipsychotic drug refilled and urged him to take them. Scotty refused.

His next stop was a nearby Holiday Inn, where he checked in for the night.

"I slept all night and feel great," he assured Kathy the next morning. "Think I'll spend another day here relaxing."

Throughout the day, I tried to reach him. The hotel did not show he had checked out, but there was no answer in his room.

Resurfacing later that day in Orlando, where his sister, Jodie, now lived, he left two messages on her answering machine.

"I'm at the Hyatt Hotel checking on enrollment in the seminary."

"I'm on my way to Fort Myers Beach to go fishing with Mom and George."

Jodie was home for his third call. This time he was calling from a hotel in Tampa.

"I'm glad you finally decided to pick up the phone, Jodie," he said. "I'm tired of talking to your damn answering machine. Got a few more important phone calls to make, then I'm hitting the road for Fort Myers Beach. We'll be seeing lots of each other while I'm at the seminary. Your brother, the minister, how does that grab you?"

The Bungalow Beach Resort in nearby Bradenton Beach was his next stop. Checking into this resort on February 3rd, he again began leaving messages for his regular psychiatrist.

"You want to continue to be my doctor, treat me as a new patient with no history of bipolar disorder," he demanded, "and keep this confidential."

The messages continued. "I'm having nightmares about demons trying to kill me... The Holy Spirit is the manic part of bipolar disorder... I'm running for president of the United States."

Late that evening, Scotty drove to a nearby convenience store, parked his car, and went inside. Slowly strolling up one aisle and down another as though he was shopping, he began to initiate conversations with other customers, offering them his meds.

Suspecting Scotty was selling drugs, the store manager called the police. Responding with two drug-sniffing dogs, the police recognized that Scotty was ill and transported him to the Manatee Glens Hospital in Bradenton. His car was later picked up at the convenience store parking lot and impounded by the police.

The following morning, George and I drove from Fort Myers Beach to the hospital in Bradenton. The Manatee Glens Hospital had no insurance requirements, received its funding from the state and county, and specialized in treating mental illness and substance abuse.

Scotty was taken from the crisis stabilization unit and escorted to the private room where we were. His physical appearance resembled a homeless person's — unkempt and reeking of body odor. Carrying an open Bible, he quoted scriptures. He hugged me, shook hands with George, and seemed surprised to see us.

"What brings you two here?"

"We came to visit you," I said. "How are you doing?"

"I'm doing just great," he replied, his trademark million-dollar smile beaming.

"They can only hold me here for 72 hours," he said confidently. "They brought me in under the Florida Baker Act, and I'm now an expert on that act."

The Baker Act is the Florida law that permits people suffering from a mental illness to be picked up and held for a hearing. It was a mere coincidence that the law's title was Scotty's last name, though he was convinced the Baker Act was named after him.

When manic, Scotty's high IQ seemed to accelerate off the charts. He had, in a short period of time, memorized a large section of the Baker Act, reciting it to us and expressing confidence that he would be released later in the day.

Scotty invited us to join him for his meeting with the doctor, but changed his mind.

"You two might say something to influence the doctor," he said, "and there's no way I'll run the risk of being committed again."

The hospital case manager met with us privately. She told us Scotty had already been placed in solitary confinement for disorderly conduct, and she felt certain the doctor would hold him over for a hearing. Being unfamiliar with the Baker Act hearing process in

Florida, we asked if we could meet with the judge so we could provide him with background information on Scotty's medical history. Somewhat taken aback by our request, she responded quickly.

"The judge is an expert on the Florida Baker Act. He's a lawyer. He's not a doctor," she said emphatically. "He's very strict with the enforcement of this act, almost always ruling in favor of the patient. He never commits patients unless they are clearly a danger to themselves or others."

"Here we go again with this 'danger to themselves or others' language," I thought. I found myself wishing that Scotty could be this judge's son for a couple of years; then, we'd see if he was still as strict with the law's enforcement.

"Perhaps you can give us some advice on another situation," I said. "Scotty's regular psychiatrist in Virginia is having difficulty communicating with your doctor. He has left several messages, but his calls are never returned."

Once again, we received a quick response.

"This hospital is unable to solicit medical information on Scotty without his permission," she explained, "and Scotty refuses to give this permission. I suggest the doctor keep calling. If the two doctors ever connect," she said, "our doctor can listen to input from the Virginia doctor, but he's prohibited from returning or initiating calls."

She angered me. Didn't she realize that Scotty's regular psychiatrist had other patients, some as ill as Scotty? He could not spend his days trying to "connect," as she put it, with the Florida physician.

It wasn't a good time to lose our cool, as George pointed out. I bit my tongue and kept my thoughts to myself, but I had a question. "How does a family such as ours get Scotty the medical treatment he so desperately needs to get well?"

"I understand and appreciate how difficult it is on families with adult members suffering from mental illness," she said, "but the laws are designed to protect the civil rights of these people."

"How about protecting the civil rights of innocent people Scotty may harm during one of his manic episodes?" I wanted to ask her. Instead, it seemed prudent to keep my thoughts to myself yet again.

Scotty's meeting with the local psychiatrist — which we were not allowed to attend — resulted in a recommendation that he be held over for a Baker Act hearing. We asked permission to attend. Once again, Scotty exercised his right to have no family in attendance.

In the days that followed, his grandiose, delusional thoughts grew worse with every conversation.

"I just talked with several partners at your law firm," Scotty told me. "They've agreed to represent me with my class action lawsuits. In fact, they told me it would be an honor to represent such a prestigious client."

I had retired from the law firm six months prior to Scotty's second breakdown. My replacement knew of my son's illness.

"Scotty, please stop calling my former employer," I pleaded. "I've told them you're ill and to ignore your calls. Please don't call them again," I begged.

"Mom, I need a big-name law firm behind me. Yours is the best."

Jumping subjects, he continued. "I'm buying property in Vienna, Virginia. That is, if Buddy hasn't completely screwed up the deal."

Leaping to yet another subject, "Guess what? It's official! I'm running for the office of president of the United States. Hillary will be my running mate. I'll be the next president. Your son, the president! How does that grab you?"

Along with others, I never understood Scotty's fixation with Hillary Clinton when manic. He always said very unkind things about her when well. Mania somehow created this close friendship between him and the former first lady.

The hearing determined that Scotty would be held for one week only and no longer. The judge requested that a family member escort him from the hospital when released, because he had no driver's license — the Brunswick County Sheriff's Office had confiscated it two weeks earlier.

Alarmed by the judge's decision and the hearing's results, Kathy spoke with the doctor.

"My brother still believes he's in the Witness Protection Program and that he will be the next president of the United States. He's so ill that one week of treatment is not going to work. He's very accomplished at beating the system. He knows how to behave at hearings and when to keep his mouth shut. I don't think the judge realizes how sick he is. Can't you do something?" she pleaded.

The doctor confided to her that the judge had actually wanted to release Scotty after the hearing, but he fought for the one-week detention.

"Your brother presents as a classic bipolar with no evidence of schizophrenia. His mania will eventually burn itself out as long as he continues to take his lithium," he explained. "Since your brother won't be completely well when we release him in a week and he has no driver's license, you'll need to line up one of your brothers to accompany him on his flight back to Virginia."

"Here we go again," I thought. The doctor was actually admitting that Scotty would not be completely well in a week, but was going to release him anyway. "Where have we heard this before? How could he do this?" I asked myself time and time again.

And then, the doctor forewarned us, "The hospital received a fax from Scotty's realtor in Virginia," he said. "It seems the Vienna property he wants to purchase is no longer available. I predict this news will cause much agitation."

Several days earlier, Buddy had been instrumental in persuading the realtor to cancel the sales contract after explaining Scotty's situation.

The doctor's prediction of "much agitation" hit the nail on the head. Scotty prepared a 23-page fax to his Virginia realtor. The realtor had accepted another contract on the $300,000 property Scotty wanted to purchase, but agreed to send him a false contract. The realtor's motive was twofold. The false contract would hopefully pacify Scotty, but, more importantly, it would also put an end to the 25 to 30 disruptive calls they received from him daily.

"Can you please call the Brunswick County sheriff's office?" Scotty asked Tricia. "Have them overnight my driver's license. I'm having one of my employees overnight my passport. I'll need both when I get out of here."

We received notification on February 14th that Scotty would be released the following day. "Scotty is 70 percent back to normal," the doctor told us.

Reiterating his previous discharge instructions that a family member must pick Scotty up and drive him to the airport, the doctor further insisted that a family member meet his flight in Virginia.

Scotty had received his passport for airport ID purposes. He still had no driver's license.

As George and I were preparing to leave for the hospital to pick Scotty up and drive him to the airport, he called in an agitated state.

"Where are you? I've been released. I'm waiting in the lobby for you," he shouted. "You two are retired, with nothing else to do. Why the hell can't you be on time?"

"We're on our way," I assured him as my nervous stomach began to churn.

Scotty had a reservation on a flight leaving Tampa at 6:45 PM, arriving at BWI Airport in Baltimore at 9:00 PM. He was irritated that his office had not booked a flight into Reagan National or Dulles Airport, both of which were located closer to his home.

We arrived at the hospital at 1:15 PM. He hadn't been released, nor was he in the lobby as he had told me. It took the staff 45 minutes to process his release and escort him to the lobby. A social worker was with him to make certain he was released to a family member. He was given several containers of medicine, which he placed in his bag.

He looked pitiful. His shoelaces had been removed during confinement, so he struggled to keep his shoes on. He was unshaven, having had no access to a razor. His clothes were tattered and he needed a haircut.

Clearly manic, having received the equivalent of only band-aid treatment, Scotty was being released in our care. "What were we thinking when we agreed to do this?" I asked myself.

The hospital in essence was saying, "Get him out of here. He's your responsibility now, not ours."

We were burdened with HIPAA, bureaucracy, cowardly physicians, rude nurses, and a world turned upside down. What next?

6. An Unforgettable, Regrettable Drive

Clearly, we had not thought things through, but it was too late to turn back. Scotty was our responsibility now.

George and I aren't doctors, but even we knew he wasn't well enough to leave the hospital. How could a doctor release such a sick person and sleep at night? We put Scotty in our car and drove away.

Several days earlier, we had located Scotty's car through the Manatee County sheriff's department. The police had picked it up on the night he was arrested at the convenience store. We drove him to the impoundment lot to retrieve the car, but stopped en route at the local Western Union office. Scotty wanted to collect the money his office had wired to pay the towing and storage charges — $480.00.

"Monopoly money," Scotty said, laughing. He paid the bill, and an attendant drove his car out of the fenced-in lot.

"God bless you, sir, and have a nice day," Scotty said, tipping the attendant $50, again referring to it as monopoly money.

The back of his Explorer overflowed with junk that he'd purchased during his travels. The car was filthy and reeked of cigar smoke and discarded fast food.

"Hold your nose, Mom," he said, climbing into the driver's seat.

"Scotty, I'm driving your car," I told him in no uncertain terms. I felt unsafe with him behind the wheel, and besides, he had no driver's license. He, of course, objected, forcing me to take advantage of the license situation. I reminded him that he had no driver's license, and that getting stopped by the police for a traffic violation would interfere with his plans to return to Virginia.

After a brief clash, he surrendered his keys and climbed into the passenger seat, pulled out a cigar, and lit it. He had purchased cigars at the cigar store next to Western Union. Knowing full well that cigar smoke offends me, he puffed away, blowing the smoke in my direction, his way of getting back at me for driving. I said nothing. I had learned to choose my battles with him.

When Scotty was arrested at the convenience store 12 days earlier, all of his personal belongings were left in his room at the Bungalow Beach Resort on Bradenton Beach. The hotel had been notified that Scotty was ill, and the manager kindly offered to pack his belongings and hold them for pickup. I drove to the hotel to collect his things; George followed in our car.

Some drives are a breeze. They're over before they begin, it seems. Other drives are unforgettable for all the wrong reasons. This short drive lasted an eternity. Choosing my words carefully, trying hard not to say anything that might provoke Scotty, I grew nervous. A knot formed in my stomach. I knew I had to project an "I'm in charge," image, while keeping his manic temperament in tow.

When he didn't like something I said, he turned the radio volume as high as it would go, put his feet on the dash, reclined in his seat, closed his eyes, and puffed away. When he, too, could no longer stand the noise, he turned the volume down. I knew better than to touch the radio.

Tired of testing my radio endurance, he moved on to updating me on his psychotic thoughts. Talking nonstop and pausing only long enough to take a breath, he rambled on and on, jumping from one subject to another.

"Mom, I know you won't believe this, but you know that FBI guy? The one who has been following me for the last ten years? Well, he was a patient at Manatee Glens. He showed me his badge! Two other patients in the Witness Protection Program with me were also FBI agents. Go figure!"

He prattled on....

"I had a police escort all the way to Florida. He was waiting for me when I left the hospital in Petersburg. Let me tell you something, these guys drive fast. I had to set my cruise control at 100 just to keep up."

And on he chattered....

"Running for president is no longer an option for me, Mom. My future wife made it clear she wants no part of being married to the president. But you know, if Hillary calls and asks me to run, I'll have to honor her request," he said seriously. "Sarah will just have to get over it."

And then he returned to one of his manic staples: my law firm.

"I'm going to sue the hell out of every mental hospital that locked me up. I've requested all my medical records. This will be the largest class action lawsuit in the history of the country. I'd like to give your law firm the business, but they won't even return my phone calls. How could you work for a firm for so many years that doesn't return important phone calls?

"My new goal in life is to champion the cause of the mentally ill," he proudly announced. "Someone has got to help those poor people. All doctors and hospitals do is pump them full of drugs. They don't need drugs. They just need to trust in the Lord. He will make them well."

He continued, "You know, I was fortunate to finally end up in a private hospital, one that made me well and treated me with dignity. State hospitals are the pits. The patients at Manatee Glens made me well, not the doctors.

"I have a confession to make," he said.

"What's that, Scotty?"

"I never swallowed any of the drugs they gave me in hospitals," he boasted. "I always spit them out when the nurse left the room."

And then his babbling turned mean-spirited.

"You know that judge at my hearing? Well, he was one weird dude," Scotty said laughing. "He had no hands. To make matters worse, one arm was missing up to the elbow. I told him, 'Hey, dude, all I want is to get out of here, smoke a cigar, and have a cold beer.' You know what he said? 'No cigars or beer for you, young man. I'm holding you over for a one-week self-medication program.'"

"I got scared," Scotty said. "I asked him why he would want to do that, but he never answered me. I was really scared, until I called my friend's father, who told me the commandant of the Marine Corps would protect me."

And then this gut-wrenching "conversation" turned back to God, as it often did.

"Your son will have his master's degree in Divinity before the end of the year," Scotty proclaimed. "How do you feel about that?" Then, answering his own question, "I think Dad will be happy. I'm still waiting on God to explain my role as a minister, you know. Guess he'll get back to me when he's ready. Sometimes he talks to me from my car radio, but maybe not today because you're in the car."

Then, an abrupt change of direction.

"I'm in deep debt with all these hospital bills. I've never been in debt! It sucks that I have to pay these bills. I wasn't even sick," he shouted. "Guess it's a good thing they accept payment plans.

"You know, Sarah postponed our wedding," he said tearfully. "She claims she needs more time to figure out how to deal with bipolar disorder."

"Scotty," I responded, "You need to be very patient with Sarah. This is a very difficult situation for her. Give her time."

"Heck, she can have all the time she needs. If she really loves me, she'll get her act together. What choice do I have?"

And then he turned on his brother.

"I'm really ticked off with Buddy, and I mean really ticked off with him this time," he yelled. "You know he's responsible for me not getting that Vienna property, and for this he will pay," he continued yelling at the top of his lungs.

I glanced over at Scotty. His face was red with anger. "Damn Buddy," he yelled, pounding the dash of his car with both fists.

"Stop it Scotty, right now! Calm down! There's no need to yell. I'm sitting right here next to you," I yelled right back at him.

I was worn to a frazzle. Having focused on my choice of words too many times that afternoon, I lost my composure.

"Don't tell me what to do!" he yelled even louder, as he began to fidget with his door handle.

Thoughts ricocheted through my head. "What if he makes a run for it? What will I do? Surely you could have kept your act together just a few more hours."

Scotty did not get out of the car because he saw the hotel just ahead, and it seemed to have a calming affect on him.

It was a welcome sight, indeed. Already annoyed with myself for having agreed to pick Scotty up at the hospital, I was now ticked off at myself for agreeing to this side trip to the hotel. We should have gone directly to the airport. To make matters worse, Scotty's personal belongings at the hotel consisted of more junk. The only items of value were the $5,000 electric guitar and amplifier system he'd purchased while staying at the Army and Navy Club. The remaining junk wouldn't even make a Goodwill donation.

After adding this junk to his overcrowded car, I began to feel reasonably comfortable that we might succeed in getting Scotty to the airport.

This comfort level vanished when he said, "I'm going swimming in the Gulf of Mexico. After that, I'm taking a dip in the hotel pool. You two just cool it."

We tried to discourage him, because of concerns about rush-hour traffic and delays in getting to the Tampa airport in time for his flight.

"You're both a couple of time freaks," he yelled as he took off for the Gulf dressed in jeans and a T-shirt.

A half hour later, he returned dripping wet, took his dip in the hotel pool, changed into some dry clothing, and got into his car with me. I drove to a restaurant parking lot near Interstate 75, while George followed in our car. We left Scotty's car in the parking lot, and the three of us drove to the airport.

During the drive, I urged Scotty to keep his mouth shut during the flight to Baltimore. "Don't talk to anyone," I pleaded. "The thoughts you shared with me will frighten other passengers. And whatever you do, Scotty, don't volunteer you were released from a mental hospital this afternoon."

I wanted to impress upon him — without making him feel that mental illness is a crime or something to be ashamed of — that most people are uncomfortable with the subject. "I don't want you to say things that will frighten other people and get you removed from the plane. If you do, Scotty," I warned him, "you may be sent back to the hospital. You'll never get home to Virginia," I continued to lecture him. "Can you please promise me you won't talk with other people on this flight?"

"I'll think about it, but can promise nothing," he replied.

Scotty thanked us for driving him to the airport, got on the plane, and was met at BWI Airport in Baltimore by one of his employees. We collected his car from the restaurant parking lot and drove it to our home in Fort Myers Beach.

The hellacious drive was over. More discord and heartbreak, of course, lay ahead. The swinging pendulum that was Scotty's life swung meanly as ever, dragging all of us along, and then a glimmer of hope surfaced, not from Scotty, but from Sarah.

7. SARAH BY HIS SIDE

Back home in Virginia, Scotty hit the ground running. His phone calls began again, a relentless stream-of-consciousness.

"I didn't keep my appointment with the psychiatrist today," he told me during the first call. "I'm going to fire that guy and never see another shrink. My regular doctor can monitor my lithium levels. I don't need a shrink," he said, shouting for emphasis.

Abruptly changing from his angry I-don't-need-a-shrink voice to a serene tone, he said, "I spent my day incorporating 25 new companies. All are incorporated in Virginia, where I grew up, not Delaware, where the tax breaks are better. What I'm telling you is highly confidential. I'd like to share this news with Sarah, but she's stressed out right now with stomach problems and I don't want to upset her."

The next day, there was a poignant call: "I haven't slept all night. I spent the entire night fighting with Sarah. I tried to talk with her roommates, but all they want to talk about is my illness. My life has become very stressful. I've reached the conclusion that nothing in this world is meant to be. I'm no longer sure Sarah is the one. I called her parents. I called my psychiatrist. I called my minister. I need help," he began to sob.

His heart-rending message brought me to tears. I called Scotty. He laughed, claimed he'd never left such a message, and assured me everything was fine. He called the next day, describing yet another fight with Sarah.

"Please call and reassure her I'm still the same sweet person she fell in love with and agreed to marry," he pleaded. "I've asked her parents to do the same."

"Sarah, you're the one who needs help," he told her the next day. "Schedule an appointment with my psychiatrist. I'm not the sick one. You are. I don't have bipolar disorder. What I have is a rare gift from God. I feel better than I've ever felt in my life."

By now, Sarah had learned it was impossible to reason with Scotty during a manic episode. He was incapable of having a rational conversation — with anyone — and his manic actions led to a lot of upheaval.

The law firm where I had previously worked in Washington, DC, notified me of an unusual phone call from a man who identified himself as my son.

"I'm faxing documents that prove my civil rights are being violated," he told the firm's receptionist. "I'm being held hostage. I need legal representation. Have your best lawyer call me immediately. This is an emergency."

A month earlier, the firm had received a similar call but ignored it, thinking it was a prank. They knew of Scotty's illness, but given the serious situation he portrayed, this time they contacted me. I apologized, told them Scotty was off his medications again, and told them to tell Scotty they had no interest in representing him.

His behavior wore people down. It became too much to take at times. Sarah gave Scotty news he didn't want to hear.

"I can't commit to a date for the wedding, or for that matter, to a wedding at all."

"Tell you what, Sarah," he said, "how about I give you 48 hours to think about it?"

He sent 24 dozen long-stem red roses to Sarah's office. When she came home from work, Scotty was there with another 24 dozen roses and a horse-drawn carriage. He ordered one dozen roses every hour

— 576 long-stem roses — and asked Sarah to "think about it." He had a limousine waiting to drive them to dinner.

Earlier in the day, Buddy telephoned the Fairfax County Crisis Control Center and described his brother's behavior. The Crisis Center agreed to send a unit to Sarah's house to evaluate Scotty. Upon arrival and initial evaluation, the crisis control team didn't think Scotty needed to be hospitalized. He showed no signs of danger to himself or others. The crisis team reminded Buddy that Virginia law requires that someone with a severe mental illness must be an "imminent danger to self or others" before the person can be involuntarily committed for treatment.

Buddy did what he had to do. He antagonized Scotty just enough to get him to show hostile behavior in the crisis control team's presence. Scotty was so ill that it took very little to accomplish this goal. Buddy got in Scotty's face and repeatedly asked him, "Why don't you hit me, Scotty?" Scotty never hit Buddy, but he pounded his fist into his palm and paced furiously in circles. That was enough. He was handcuffed and transported to Mount Vernon Hospital, where a hearing was scheduled.

Kathy, Buddy, Tricia, Sarah, and her sister attended the hearing. It disturbed Scotty to see so many family members gathered. He feared that all five were there to testify against him. Rather than risk involuntary commitment, he voluntarily committed himself for five days. The judge actually tried to talk Scotty out of his decision.

"But Mr. Baker," he said, "you're entitled to a hearing."

"No thank you, judge," he responded ever so politely. "I want to commit myself."

The attending physician later confided that this judge had a track record of being very liberal and had never involuntarily committed anyone; Scotty's committing himself was a blessing. Otherwise, the judge no doubt would have released him.

Kathy, Buddy, and Tricia met with Scotty immediately after the hearing. Scotty was so angry with Buddy that he slugged him with his fist, not once, but twice. Because Scotty assaulted his brother, he fell into the category of "imminent danger to others," enabling us to have him involuntarily committed for treatment.

That afternoon, he was transferred to the Northern Virginia Mental Health Institute in nearby Falls Church. A staff member was assigned to watch him around the clock, a standard precaution for patients who have assaulted someone. The family requested that the hospital do mouth checks.

Throughout his confinement, Scotty managed his company and conducted business as usual. He persuaded the staff and his doctor to let him use a hospital conference room with a telephone as his office. His assistant, Joe, made daily trips to this "hospital office" with contracts and business documents for Scotty's review.

In the meantime, Buddy visited Scotty's Fairfax office to check on things. He learned that most of the employees were looking for other jobs. Scotty's behavior made them uncomfortable. He also discovered that Scotty had rented an apartment for the homeless man he met on the street and was paying the rent. Scotty wanted to hire this person, but Joe and other employees agreed the man was unemployable. Scotty felt the least he could do was pay his rent.

At the same time, the business appeared to be disintegrating, a lot of money was being spent. Buddy found the receipt for the 48 dozen roses — $2,300. The horse-drawn carriage and limo added another $800. Scotty had written a $10,000 check to the Clinton Defense Fund, but Buddy couldn't confirm that Scotty had ever mailed the check. Writing a check to the Clinton Defense Fund was something a well Scotty would never have done.

Scotty was now responsible for all hospital charges. The daily rate at this latest facility was $515. His health insurance had provided coverage for a maximum of 30 days per year for inpatient mental health care. Scotty, released on March 20, 2000, was responsible for the 24 days of hospital charges that exceeded the 30-day maximum. At $515 per day, he owed the hospital $12,360.

During this 80-day manic episode, the following hospitals treated Scotty:

1) Sibley Hospital, Washington, DC — four days
2) Georgetown University Hospital, Washington, DC — two days
3) Poplar Springs Hospital, Petersburg, Virginia — nine days
4) Manatee Glens Hospital, Bradenton, Florida — 13 days
5) Northern Virginia Mental Health Institute, Falls Church, Virginia — 26 days

These hospitals and the insurance companies that control them lead me to an important aside. Nine months, nine months fraught with fear, remained in 2000. Should Scotty become mentally ill again, he'd shoulder all inpatient charges. The financial burdens from his breakdown and use of all allotted inpatient mental health care for the year — as defined by his mercenary insurance company — worried him and us.

Compounding the misery created by the HIPAA bureaucrats, insurers play an unacceptable role in the treatment of the mentally ill; they should be ashamed, but they aren't. Just the opposite, in fact. These bureaucratic dolts, smug, ensconced, and calling the shots, penalize mentally ill people and their families. If you have a brain tumor, for instance, your medical insurance does not place a 30-day cap on your inpatient care. Suffer bipolar disorder, however, and insurance companies cover only a very limited hospital stay. Why the disparity?

It's far more cost-effective to keep a mentally ill patient hospitalized until well. To release them prematurely harms the patient and requires the family to start all over again with the commitment and treatment process at another hospital, in another city, perhaps another state.

You never know what waits down the road. Scotty's sad story and mine could become yours. In fact, for many, it will. Something like 15 to 18 percent of Americans, including nearly 10 million children, have a diagnosable mental disorder. These disorders occur from childhood to old age in men and women alike. No socioeconomic group is free from the sting of mental illness. One out of every ten Americans will experience some disability from a mental health disorder. According to NAMI, mental illness affects one in four individuals. A diagnosable mental illness affects 12 percent of American children under the age of 18. The bottom line is clear. If all Americans are to receive fair and equitable health care, insurance discrimination for mental health services must end.

A start has been made. Congress passed the Mental Health Parity Act in 1996. Concerns about the adequacy of insurance benefits and quality of care for the mentally ill drove many states to require equal coverage for both mental health and medical conditions. The law has not been that effective. Under the act, even those insurers who offer both physical and mental health services can still impose other coverage limits on mental health benefits. Limits can include higher co-payment and other coinsurance requirements that are larger than those for physical health care. Treatment limits can restrict patient access to adequate mental health treatment. It's time for Congress to revisit the issue and pass laws requiring insurance companies to treat mental illness the same as any other illness. It's time for insurers to drop their tricky terms and cagey language.

Though the Mental Health Parity Act is progress — a baby step in the right direction, if you will — loopholes exist for states and employers. Even though full insurance coverage may be available for a mentally ill person, all too often they're too ill to realize they're sick; thus, they refuse treatment. The sad reality is that some ill individuals need to be forced to take treatment. The real problem comes down to treatment laws in each of the states. These laws need amending. Judges should be required to consider relevant family member testimony in involuntary commitment hearings. The laws should let family members directly petition for treatment. Something must be done.

The implications of untreated mental illness prove staggering to the individual, the individual's family, and society. A litany of ills results from this particular failure of our health care system: school dropouts, lost wages, homelessness, criminalization, and death. Scotty became unemployable as a direct result of non-treatment. We looked into Medicare and Medicaid to subsidize his care.

And so taxpayers — you and I — foot the bill to care for individuals disabled by a treatable illness. The Treatment Advocacy Center is the only organization that works at the legislative level to eliminate barriers to timely and effective treatment for people with severe mental illness.

Following Scotty's release from the Northern Virginia Mental Health Institute, he took several weeks to rest and cope with the events of the last 80 days. He recalled with much embarrassment every detail of what had transpired during his latest manic episode, and it was difficult for him. For Scotty, the word "embarrassment" took on a new meaning with this illness.

Sarah visited him throughout his confinement and was a real trooper. He was so lucky to have her. With her loving support and encouragement, Scotty struggled, but eventually moved on with his life. He saw his psychiatrist regularly, took his lithium, and managing his illness became a top priority in his life.

One of the side effects of lithium is weight gain that can be rather substantial. Scotty weighed approximately 195 pounds before he started taking lithium in January 1994. His weight gradually increased from 195 to 235 pounds, and in June 2000, he was diagnosed with type II diabetes. At six feet three inches and 235 pounds, Scotty was a large man.

According to NAMI, "Not only can weight gain lead to diabetes II and cardiovascular disease, but being overweight is also a leading cause of medication non-adherence."

Some patients stop taking lithium to control their weight. We feared Scotty might do the same.

This additional weight gain, especially noticeable in his face, particularly his jaws and neck, made him extremely self-conscious. Though encouraged and advised by his doctor to exercise regularly and eat a healthy diet, Scotty paid little attention until diabetes forced him to go on a very strict diet. Now, in addition to periodic blood work to monitor his lithium level, he also had to monitor his blood sugar.

In spite of Scotty's mental and physical health problems, Sarah and his relationship flourished, and on a chilly day in March 2001, they were married in a beautiful ceremony. One of her conditions for the marriage was that if she or any member of his family felt that he was becoming manic again, he would immediately admit himself to a hospital for treatment. What Sarah did not realize or understand at the time was that when manic, Scotty was incapable of keeping promises.

Grateful to have her by his side, Scotty worked hard at his marriage and managing his illness. He worked diligently to put the pieces back together at his company, but unfortunately, failed. Business opportunities for PTSI dried up, and the decline of his company occurred in conjunction with the bursting of the dot-com bubble.

Joe, his last remaining employee, left PTSI in November 2001, after recognizing that Scotty no longer possessed his former boundless energy, contagious enthusiasm, and drive to succeed.

Scotty was forced to close the office shortly thereafter and accept a job with a non-profit organization.

Losing the company you've worked so hard to establish, plus dealing with bipolar disorder and the maintenance required to manage both this illness and diabetes can tax any marriage. Sarah, to her credit, played a supportive role from day one.

She and Scotty made a great team. It takes a very special person to marry someone with a mental illness, and Sarah was indeed that very special person. She'd seen him in action during his second breakdown and married him anyway. She did this with the support and encouragement of her family. They, too, loved Scotty and welcomed him into the family. Yes, he had a mental illness, but his many other fine qualities far outweighed their concerns about another manic episode.

Sarah and Scotty were enjoying an active, happy life together. Managing his illness was a team effort. She involved herself in his treatment program and occasionally accompanied him to doctor visits. Both were gainfully employed and settling into a new home they purchased in nearby Oakton. Best of all, Sarah was by his side during what would prove to be a peaceful interlude.

8. THE GATHERING STORM

Anyone can have a bad day, certainly a bad moment. And everyone acts out of character now and then. Generally it's no cause for alarm, but with bipolar sufferers, an out-of-character moment can herald the onset of Hell itself.

Not one of us was prepared when another round of signs of mania struck in September 2002. Only two and a half years had passed since the last episode. How could this be happening again so soon?

Simple... a weekend getaway went awry.

Sarah and Scotty had planned to join Sarah's sister and friends for a relaxing weekend on the Outer Banks in Corolla, North Carolina. Scotty decided to get an early start on the weekend by leaving Thursday evening. That forced Sarah, unable to take Friday off, to make the six-hour drive by herself on Friday night. Being inconsiderate of Sarah was out of character for Scotty. That was a shot across our bow.

Throughout the weekend, Scotty's abnormal behavior strengthened its hold on him, unnerving others. He verbally confronted one of the women in the group when he went into her bedroom without permission, yet another action that was out of character for Scotty. Apparently aware of his behavior, he turned to Sarah.

"Sarah, I need some time alone so I can relax. I'm having trouble relaxing," something he told her several times.

One evening, they watched the movie *A Beautiful Mind*, based on a true story about John Nash, a Nobel laureate in economics who suffered from schizophrenia. The film takes up the story in Nash's early years at Princeton as he develops an extraordinary idea that will revolutionize mathematics. The movie's storyline, though, deals with mental illness. Nash develops paranoid schizophrenia and suffers delusional episodes. He watches in agony as his wife and friends suffer because of his illness. Nash, like Scotty, believed he possessed high-level information, in his case, top-secret Soviet codes. Nash believed the Soviets were trying to kidnap him to recapture their information. It disappointed Scotty when he realized that Nash was mentally ill, and that the Soviets were not really trying to kill him.

"Sarah," he said with concern after watching this movie, "I've got to start taking better care of myself mentally."

As for his early departure on Thursday, leaving Sarah to drive down alone, Scotty confessed to Sarah, "Federal agents were following me again, and I didn't want to put your life in danger by traveling with me."

"Scotty, you've got to schedule an appointment with your doctor as soon as we get home," she told him, hoping it wasn't too late to nip this episode in the bud. He did as she requested.

Prior to the appointment, Kathy called the doctor to give him a heads-up. She enjoyed a good relationship with this psychiatrist, who had been treating Scotty since his first episode.

When Scotty learned what Kathy had done, he exploded.

"Mind your own damn business and stay the fuck out of my life!"

A few hours later, calling to apologize to Kathy for his behavior, he lost it again.

"Everyone in this family needs to worry about their own shit, and you need to back off."

With this episode's onset on the heels of 9/11 and the increased security in Washington, DC, I grew increasingly concerned about Scotty's previous fixation with the White House and the president. Worrying about situations I cannot control has always been a problem for me. I feared he might climb the White House fence and be shot. Each time the news media reported an incident involving someone trying to get into the White House, I waited for the individual to be identified by name, thinking, "Oh, please, may this person not be Scotty."

I called the Secret Service, needing assurance that its agents were trained to distinguish a terrorist from a mentally ill person. I was upfront, told them about Scotty's illness, his previous attempts to gain access to the White House, his fixation with the president, and my fear that they might shoot him.

The Secret Service confirmed that the name, Scott Baker, was not among their records, which meant that he always left the premises when told to do so. They assured me their agents were trained to deal with mentally ill people. My comfort level somewhat restored, I nonetheless worried about the danger associated with Scotty's White House and presidential obsession in the post-9/11 environment.

Despite his outbursts of late, Scotty kept his doctor's appointment, but the outcome was alarming.

"That damn doctor doesn't know what the hell he's talking about," he told Sarah. "I'll get a second opinion."

Sarah checked his medicine container and verified that the correct number of pills was missing, but had no way of knowing if Scotty had taken them or flushed them down the toilet. The previous week, she'd asked him to take his medicine in her presence and he'd gotten so angry that she concluded it wasn't worth the controversy. Firsthand experience with bipolar disorder taught Sarah to choose her battles with Scotty during manic episodes.

Unaware that their son-in-law was ill again, Sarah's parents and brother dropped by for a visit. They were scheduled to leave on a two-week trip to Europe, and Sarah didn't want to worry them or make them feel obligated to cancel their trip. She did her best to conceal her husband's behavior.

Scotty surprised her when he invited her brother to take a look at a new XM receiver in his car. Her brother assumed they would sit in the car and listen in the driveway. Instead, Scotty started his engine, backed out the driveway, and sped off.

"We're going to a party," he shouted, accelerating to 70 in a 35-mile-per-hour speed zone.

"Scotty is either drunk or high on something," Sarah's brother thought, quickly fastening his seatbelt.

The next thing he knew, they were, in fact, at a party, a large outdoor community party with lots of children. Realizing that Scotty's behavior was downright bizarre, he just wanted to return to his sister's house. To his dismay, Scotty got out of the car, chitchatted with people, drank a couple of their beers, got back in the car, and drove back home. Sarah's brother knew his brother-in-law had bipolar disorder, but this was the first time he'd witnessed Scotty in action.

Later that day, Scotty sent family members the following email:

George Pacharis
_____

From	Scott C Baker [sbaker@createhope com]
Sent:	Sunday, September 29, 2002 5:40 PM
To:	
Cc:	
Subject:	FYI

Holy Spirit

Matthew 3:11 tells us that John the Baptist baptized with water for repentance But afterward, Jesus being more powerful, will baptize you with the Holy Spirit and with fire.

Acts 1:8 tells us "But you will receive power when the Holy Spirit comes on you; and you will be my witnesses in Jerusalem, and in all Judea and Samaria, and to the ends of the earth.

The Holy Spirit empowers us to be effective witnesses. A witness is one who not only tells the truth, but also lives the truth. It is impossible to be an effective witness for Christ apart from the power and presence of the Holy Spirit.

Don't worry about me, I will be fine. Have faith.

Love You,
Scott Clovis Baker

Scotty was exceedingly religious during his manic episodes. This email was tantamount to a Code Red alert: It confirmed just how ill Scotty had become. Watching the illness take over his mind broke our hearts.

"You're fired!" Scotty told his longtime psychiatrist. "Don't ever call me or my wife again," he yelled into the phone.

The doctor responded by letter the same day.

I received your phone message today stating I'm no longer your doctor and requesting I not call you or your wife. I'll honor your decision; however, I sincerely hope you will continue the treatment which is so necessary for your health and well-being, and that you will find another psychiatrist with whom you can work effectively.

The doctor enclosed a list of other psychiatrists in the area. As we later learned, he planned to retire soon anyway, and Scotty would have been forced to find another doctor regardless.

When manic, Scotty's body required little or no sleep. He could go for days without sleep, yet maintain an energy level surpassing that of his entire family combined. Sarah had no choice but to endure his nightly ritual of loud telephone conversations with friends, neighbors, or anybody who would talk with him at two or three o'clock in the morning. Scotty never considered that his wife had to get up for work the next morning. By now, Scotty had lost his job. Sarah was the breadwinner.

As she was getting dressed for work one morning, Sarah turned down the radio volume in their bedroom after Scotty had turned it up very loud.

"You ever do that again," he yelled, "and I'll tear your arm out of its socket and sell it!"

This was the first time he'd threatened Sarah with bodily harm.

Later that morning, Scotty showed up unannounced at Chris's house. He helped himself to a beer, then two more, literally inhaling all three. He talked nonstop, complaining about Sarah and describing all the Secret Service agents who were following him. When Chris cut off his beer supply, Scotty left, got into his car, and drove off at high speed.

In Scotty's bipolar world, the Secret Service agents continued to track him throughout the following day.

"I wasn't sure they'd been following me for the last couple of months," he said, "until today, when cars actually pulled over on the side of the road to give me the right-of-way." Lie low and wait, were his instructions from the agents.

"I'll be the next president of the United States, and this time, George W. will be my running mate—Baker/Bush," he announced with pride. "How does that grab you?"

"Kathy, plan on bringing your children to the next White House Easter Egg Roll."

The next day, he seemed completely normal during an hour-long telephone conversation with Kathy. A few minutes later, mania dispersed this refreshingly normal disposition.

"Sarah, I want you out of this house," he yelled. "I'm doing what God tells me to do, and you're not supporting me."

Sarah, concerned about her safety, was quick to comply. She collected some personal effects and went to her parents' house in Springfield. A short time after her departure, the neighbor across the street saw Scotty back his car out of the driveway at high speed, ending up in the ditch across the street. Had there been cars in his path, he would have hit them. Several young children were playing nearby. A tragedy could easily have occurred.

Late that evening, the same neighbor observed Scotty in his bare feet, wearing nothing but boxer shorts, running his lawn mower over the landscape lighting along the walkway to the front door. Word of Scotty's reckless and weird behavior spread throughout the neighborhood creating concern.

Destroying the landscape lighting was Scotty's attempt to darken his yard. He had already removed all the light bulbs from his house. He didn't want federal agents to see inside his house. He felt safe in a dark house.

Normal life just did not exist. My heart went out to Sarah. She was trying to maintain some semblance of order in her life and work while dealing with Scotty's illness, which was taking an obvious toll on her. We arranged to meet for lunch on a Saturday. I drove from my home in West River, Maryland, to her parents' house. They were still in Europe. We went out for lunch and agreed not to talk about bipolar disorder.

When we returned to her parents' house, a message awaited us on the answering machine from the Fairfax County police, requesting she call them as soon as possible. Shaken and fearing the worst, Sarah nervously returned the call.

"Mrs. Baker, we received a call from your husband requesting a bulletproof vest," the police officer told Sarah. "Your husband claims he needs this vest for protection from federal agents who are trying to kill him," he continued. "We dispatched a patrol car to his house and offered to transport him to the hospital, but he refused. The purpose of my call is to make certain you know your husband is very ill."

"Thank you, officer," Sarah responded. "Please ignore my husband's call. He's bipolar and off his meds."

Sarah was such a lady and so polite to the police officer. I wanted in the worst way to grab the phone, but didn't want to embarrass her.

I would have told the officer, "You're damn right we know he's ill. But guess what? We're helpless. Virginia laws prevent us from getting him treated. Would you believe we have to wait until he hurts himself or another person before this state will consider him sick enough to treat involuntarily? I hope my son calls you every hour for weeks on end with all sorts of weird requests and that you have to dispatch a patrol car to his house with each call!"

The frustration proved maddening. I kept my thoughts to myself. The commitment laws in Virginia were not the police officer's fault. He was just doing his job.

Sarah needed additional clothing and personal items from her house, but didn't want to go alone in case Scotty was there. I offered to go with her and telephoned George to let him know I would be delayed getting home. He grew concerned for our safety and asked Chris, who lived 20 minutes away, to meet us there. Scotty's car was not in the driveway when we arrived, and we both breathed a sigh of relief. The front door was wide open and the house was trashed, with debris scattered everywhere. The front door was open because the doorframe had been destroyed and the drywall smashed. The door would not close.

The kitchen, extremely warm, had its oven on at 375 degrees. Fortunately, Scotty had left no food inside.

We found a manila folder with a note written on it in Scotty's handwriting that read, "Don't tread on me. No Treason. No Trespassing. All U.S. rights reserved. Baker vs. White House and United States Supreme Court." Nearby, we also found a scrap of paper with the White House telephone number in his handwriting and a blank United Methodist membership card, on which Scotty had written "United States Commander in Chief" in the space designated for the member's name.

A large butcher knife lay on the dining room table. Next to the knife lay a check written and signed by Scotty for the amount of $50,000, payable to his minister.

We quickly packed Sarah's clothing and left. Chris returned to his house. As Sarah and I were en route to her parents' house, her cell phone rang. It was their minister. Scotty had just spent an hour at her church office. He'd come in with a large knife, but fortunately relinquished it when she asked him to give it to her. She called the Fairfax County Crisis Control Center, which dispatched a crisis control team to evaluate Scotty. Scotty, in his delusional stupor, even with the knife that should have proven he was not normal, convinced these people that he was fine. In their infinite wisdom, they concluded he was not an "imminent danger to self or others" and allowed him to leave.

"Unbelievable!" I was so weary of this law. Scotty had become a pro at convincing people in authority that he was not a threat to himself or others, but these people, supposedly, were trained to deal with the mentally ill and should have recognized a snow job. How many people show up unannounced on a Saturday night at their minister's office with a knife? Not only was Scotty well versed in

Virginia law for court-ordered treatment, he had also researched the commitment laws in every other state along the East Coast.

After leaving his minister's office, the Fairfax County police picked Scotty up for yelling in his neighbor's yard. The police transported him to Mount Vernon Hospital. A 7:00 AM hearing was scheduled for October 7.

While the police were taking Scotty into custody, several neighbors insisted that the police search the house for Sarah. They feared she was inside the house injured, perhaps dead, because Scotty had told them, "My wife has gone to the dark side." Of course, Sarah was safe at her parents' house.

The following day, Chris returned to the house to photograph the damage for use at the October 7 hearing. He also collected the White House items and the $50,000 check Scotty had written to his minister.

Kathy, Tricia, Chris, Sarah, Sarah's brother, Scotty's minister, and George and I attended the hearing. We had to be on the road by 5:00 AM to negotiate the Washington, DC, rush hour traffic for the 7:00 AM hearing. A public defender, paid for by the taxpayers of the State of Virginia, represented Scotty. We had no legal representation.

In the small hearing room, George and I sat directly behind Scotty and his lawyer, and their conversation drifted back to us.

"I'm pleading my own case, I'm good at this," Scotty told his lawyer at least half a dozen times.

"Just keep your mouth shut," the lawyer repeated each time.

Chris took the lead for the family and described Scotty's behavior during the past few weeks. He showed the judge photographs of the damage Scotty had done to the front door of his house, the White House evidence, and the $50,000 check he had written to his minister.

Scotty's lawyer responded straightaway:

"It's not against the law for someone to destroy his own property or write down the White House telephone number," he said, "and it's certainly not against the law to write a large check to your minister."

Giving this lawyer-automaton of scripted responses a look of disdain, Chris continued. He showed the judge a statement from Scotty's neighbor, who couldn't take off work and testify in person on such short notice. The neighbor had witnessed Scotty's backing his car out of his driveway at a high rate of speed and ending up in the ditch across the street. Chris explained that young children were playing in the area at the time, and their parents — "

— "Did this neighbor call the police?" The attorney interrupted Chris before he could tell the judge how Scotty's reckless behavior concerned the children's parents.

"No," Chris replied.

"Then he could not have been too concerned," the lawyer said with sarcasm.

Sarah's brother described his experience when Scotty was driving 70 miles an hour in a 35-mile per hour speed zone with no seatbelt.

"Did you call the police when you got out of the car?" the lawyer asked.

"No," he answered.

"Obviously, you weren't too scared," the lawyer responded, once again sarcastically.

Kathy told the judge she knew her brother had been driving erratically at high speed.

"Did you actually witness my client's erratic driving?" he asked.

Kathy, not one to lie, panicked and responded "yes" to the lawyer, and later recalled how sad she felt to have to lie to get Scotty treated.

Sarah described Scotty's threat to harm her when she'd turned the radio volume down.

Once again, Scotty's lawyer asked his standard question. "Did you call the police?"

"No."

This lawyer, whom we loathed, simply smiled.

Scotty's attending psychiatrist then testified. The doctor told the judge he had spent several hours with Mr. Baker, concluded he was very ill, in need of immediate treatment, and recommended involuntary commitment.

The judge reviewed his notes for a few moments and ruled that Scotty was not an "imminent danger to self or others." Scotty was released yet again.

This hearing process frustrated us beyond description. As we left the hearing room, Chris slammed the door on the lawyer's hand. Though out of character for Chris, it represented the anger and frustration we felt toward the judge and especially this lawyer, who was only there to collect his fee from Virginia taxpayers. He could not have cared less about Scotty's well-being or the innocent victims in his path.

The family gathered in the hospital cafeteria to rehash the inequities of the system and discuss what we could have done differently. Scotty's lawyer approached our table and reprimanded Chris for slamming the door on his hand. We apologized, but explained he had no idea what it was like to be in our helpless situation.

Apparently feeling some compassion toward us, he suggested we have legal representation at future hearings and tossed the card of a lawyer he recommended on our table.

"I'd like to represent you myself," he said, "but since Mr. Baker is now my client, it would be a conflict of interest."

Kathy and Tricia left the cafeteria in a last-minute effort to persuade Scotty to commit himself, but Scotty had already gone. He was seen leaving the hospital on foot, wearing no shoes.

Though Sarah had the foresight to confiscate his car keys, Scotty borrowed a car under false pretenses and resurfaced the following day in Raleigh, North Carolina. Ann Hancock, an old neighbor from our Springfield neighborhood who had retired and was living in the Raleigh area received a call from him at 1:45 AM.

"I'm at the fire station down the street and need a place to stay for the night," Scotty said. "Can you help me out?"

Ann knew that Scotty was bipolar, realized he was ill, and called his youngest sister Jodie for guidance. Jodie, her husband, and their two children had relocated from Orlando and lived in nearby Cary.

"Can you please call my mom?" Jodie asked.

At 2 AM, our phone rang. Ann explained why she was calling. "I'm so glad to know where he is and that he's safe," I told her, "but very sorry to get you involved at this hour of the morning."

"It's okay," she assured me with much compassion. "We want to help Scotty, but we're not sure how to handle the situation and don't want to say or do the wrong thing."

Briefly describing how ill he was and updating her on the previous day's hearing, I asked her to help get Scotty to a hospital. She assured me they'd do their best. Their son and Scotty had been childhood friends and had maintained their friendship since elementary school.

Her husband, Dave, and son, Jeff, drove to the fire station. Scotty, of course, refused to go to the hospital. In his condition, they were uncomfortable taking him to their house for the night, so they drove him to a nearby hotel.

Wanting no part of a hotel "overrun" with federal agents, Scotty insisted, "I've got to get to Atlanta to escape from the federal agents who are trying to kill me! I can't stay here."

Dave, attempting to convince him to remain at the hotel, said, "Scotty, I just saw the federal agents heading toward Atlanta. That city is not a safe place for you tonight. You need to stay here where you'll be safe."

Reluctantly, Scotty agreed.

The hotel wouldn't accept Scotty's MasterCard, so Dave kindly paid for the overnight accommodation. He noted that Scotty also had a Visa card and $12 in cash.

Later that morning, Dave and Jeff returned to the hotel, picked Scotty up, and drove him to their house. By this time, he had a large wad of bills in his possession, apparently having used his Visa card at an ATM.

Dave contacted the Wake County Mental Health Services in Raleigh and arranged for the county's crisis control center to evaluate Scotty at his home. I provided insurance information and a list of current medications. The crisis team concluded that Scotty was "a danger to self," and transported him to the Holly Hill Mental Hospital in Raleigh, where he was admitted.

At long last, Scotty was going to get the treatment he needed to be healed and rejoin society. How pitiful that it had come to this. He had to get so sick and be declared a "danger to self" before we could get him involuntarily treated.

At this point, George was concerned about my health. "Dottie, I know you're very worried about Scotty. So am I, but his illness is taking a noticeable toll on your health. This is the first time I've ever seen you look your age. You don't look well. You'll be of no use to him in this condition, and you must back off."

George was right. I wasn't sleeping and was having difficulty focusing. I couldn't eat, and weight was falling off me. I had to get a grip on myself and made a concerted effort to do so.

A hearing was scheduled at the hospital. Considered a "flight risk" because of his previous escape history, the doctor placed Scotty on high security with a one-on-one hospital staff employee assigned to watch him day and night.

Sarah drove to Raleigh for the hearing. Based upon his doctor's recommendation and the testimony from Sarah and Dave, the judge offered Scotty the opportunity to voluntarily commit himself for 21 days. He, of course, refused, whereupon the judge involuntarily committed him for up to 30 days with forced medications.

"Your honor," Scotty said, "You have a fine hospital here, but I request a transfer to a mental hospital in Fairfax, Virginia."

"Mr. Baker," the judge responded, "I'll honor your request and approve a transfer to a Fairfax hospital, but you're responsible for finding a hospital that will accept you as a patient and for arranging a secure ambulance transport. Would you like to pursue this course of action?"

Scotty, deflated by the judge's response, chose to remain at Holly Hill Hospital.

What a difference in the outcome of a hearing in North Carolina, compared with Virginia, where the laws protected Scotty's right to remain psychotic. It was so refreshing at long last to have this North Carolina judge listen to a doctor's recommendation and rule to help Scotty get well instead of releasing him to continue his flight from the "federal agents" of his bipolar world.

The involuntary commitment law in North Carolina is not as restrictive as the Virginia law. It also reads "danger to self/others," but "includes reasonable probability of suffering serious physical debilitation from the inability to, without assistance, either exercise self-control, judgment, and discretion in conduct and social relations; or satisfy need for nourishment, personal or medical care, shelter, or self-protection and safety."

Sarah did not return to Raleigh to visit Scotty. She had made it clear after his second breakdown that if he ever fled again when manic, she would not visit him.

Wasting no time in taking advantage of having his sister, Jodie, nearby, Scotty began calling her nonstop. His first call was to request a certain brand of cigarettes. Scotty never smoked except when hospitalized. He quickly figured out that smokers enjoy privileges that non-smokers do not. They're allowed unlimited breaks outdoors in the smoking area, while non-smokers are not.

Jodie purchased the cigarettes and delivered them to the hospital. She had her two preschool children with her, so made no attempt to visit him. When she got home, Scotty had left 12 messages, all demanding a certain type of Cuban cigar.

She called him. "No more deliveries, Scotty," she told him emphatically.

This angered him, and he called her throughout the night.

"Pick up the damn phone, Jodie," he yelled time and time again. "I know you're there."

She turned off her answering machine, thinking Scotty would eventually give up and go to bed. Not so. Realizing what she had done, he accelerated his nonstop calling, letting the phone ring 40 to 50 times before hanging up and starting again. Jodie took the phone off the hook so she and her family could get some sleep.

Several days later, she turned the answering machine back on. Scotty's demands started all over again.

"I'm the president of the United States; I'm in the middle of a very important meeting with my cabinet. We're hungry. I need a pizza delivery, Jodie. You let me down before. Don't let me down this time."

"I need more cigarettes, Jodie," he demanded in another message, "and I'm still waiting for those Cuban cigars."

During the last call, his language was so obnoxious that she turned the answering machine off, refusing to take any further calls.

Stressed out as we all were from coping with Scotty's hospitalization, life went on in our family. Chris was married.

The car Scotty borrowed was still in Raleigh. Jodie drove it back to Virginia when she went to the wedding, while her husband and children followed in their car.

Chris had tracked the borrowed car to a Ford dealership in Fairfax. The manager of the dealership's service department was a high school friend of both Scotty and Chris. Scotty had shown up at the dealership shortly after his release from Mount Vernon Hospital.

"I've donated my car to charity," Scotty had explained to his high school friend. "I'm getting a new one next week, but need wheels for a few days. Can you help me out?"

"I specifically recall that day because Scotty was acting a little unusual," his friend explained to Chris, "but I've loaned your brother cars before, and there was never a problem. I had no idea he was bipolar. I could lose my job if he doesn't return that car."

Sarah confirmed that Scotty often borrowed cars during a manic episode, even when he had access to his own, because he feared it had been bugged by the Secret Service or FBI. He frequently drove rental cars for the same reason.

The high school friend was relieved and appreciative when Jodie returned the borrowed car. George and I subsequently stopped by the dealership to apologize for the incident and thank the owner for not filing charges against Scotty. He was not only understanding but very sympathetic.

Soon after the wedding, Sarah received an alarming progress report from Scotty's doctor.

"I'm happy to report your husband is showing significant signs of improvement," he informed her, "and there's a possibility I can discharge him on or before October 28."

The doctor, I'm sure, thought this would be welcome news for Sarah and her husband's family.

It was terrible news. The doctor didn't know that Scotty had continued to share delusional thoughts with family members.

Apprehensive that an October 28 discharge date would be premature, Sarah faxed the doctor recent examples of Scotty's delusional thinking.

1) "I've been committed to 12 different mental institutions and managed to never take my medicine," he told his father-in-law.

2) "My telephones are bugged and federal agents monitor all my conversations," he confided in Tricia.

3) "There are so many unbelievable miracles that have transpired during the past few weeks. I want to share them with you, but can't because federal agents listen to all my phone calls," he told Kathy.

4) "The Secret Service has selected me to be one of their drivers, and my first assignment is in Atlanta," he told Dave.

5) "I'm a messenger of God; President Bush has a special assignment for me; I have top-secret information about the DC sniper who went on the shooting rampage killing ten people. I have a personal relationship with the National Security Agency, and I've been instructed by federal agents to lie low with Sarah and my doctor," he informed Tricia.

"My husband," Sarah further alerted the doctor, "will never share these thoughts with people in authority who might be in a position to extend his hospital stay. But as a concerned wife, I fear a premature discharge will negate all our efforts to date in keeping him hospitalized. My husband, as you are no doubt aware, is very anxious to be released. He will say anything to achieve this objective and is extremely accomplished at controlling himself in the presence of doctors and hospital staff, portraying himself as a model patient.

"This is his third manic episode," Sarah continued. "During his most recent breakdown, which began in December 1999, he was admitted for short periods of time to four hospitals. It took two months before he was finally placed in a fifth hospital that would keep him long enough to permit recovery.

"During his second episode, he actually escaped from two secure facilities and was released from others before he was well, only to be committed again. Based upon past experience, my husband will not be ready for an outpatient treatment program by October 28. He's currently in a safe environment, and if you release him prematurely, he will only repeat his previous pattern of hospital revolving-door admissions, requiring a longer period of time to get well.

"Please," she found herself begging the doctor, "continue his treatment long enough to sufficiently stabilize him so he can cope with and benefit from an effective recovery program on his own in an unsupervised environment. To release him before this is accomplished," she pointed out, "will not only be very harmful to Scotty, but it will require his family to start all over again with the commitment and treatment process at another hospital, in another city, and perhaps even in another state."

I was proud of Sarah. Her fax gave the doctor more insight into the severity of Scotty's illness. A new release date of November 4, 2002, was agreed upon. Buddy picked up his brother and drove him home. Sarah elected to remain at her parents' house, but visited Scotty in the evenings when she got off work.

Life continued to serve up stress, even during the calmer days. The truth is that nothing involving a bipolar family makes for an easy day. Laws that handcuffed the family, along with Scotty's skillful manipulation of the experts, made for great heaps of frustration.

In the months to come, a power struggle would unfold, one attempting to chart new legal territory, one holding the power to protect Scotty from himself. As well, a heartbreaking issue would surface: the sad possibility that a child of Scotty's might inherit bipolar disorder.

9. An End Run around the Law

Scotty's violent behavior throughout this most recent breakdown was troublesome. He displayed more violence than during previous episodes, and I began to worry about his safety, the safety of our family, and beyond that, the safety of innocent people.

His pattern of behavior with every episode was predictable. First, the hypomanic phase with utopian feelings that would take him to a world all his own, a world that I'm told feels so good one does not want to return to reality. Scotty once described his hypomanic state to me as "the most awesome feeling in the world." During this phase, he would stop taking his medicine, bringing on full-blown mania. At this point, his family was forced to put their lives on hold and deal with the trials and tribulations of getting a severely mentally ill adult involuntarily treated.

Neurotic religious beliefs dominated every episode. He was a Prophet of God. Communications from God were transmitted over his car radio.

Grandiose thoughts, feelings of power and importance were the norm. He was either running for the office of president or was actually the president of the United States. Federal agents were trying to assassinate him. He possessed top-secret information that would bring down prominent people in our government, and his phones and email were monitored.

Scotty, age 6

Chris (age 11), Jodie (age 8), Scotty (age 10)

Chris (age 15), Scotty (age 14)

Scotty (age 17)

Scotty (age 18)

Buddy, Kathy, Tricia, Chris, Scotty
Jodie
1991

Buddy, Kathy, Tricia, Chris, Scotty
Jodie
1996

Scotty and Sarah on their wedding day
March 3, 2001

Jodie, Scotty, Kathy, Chris, Tricia
Buddy, Dottie
February 2002

Scotty and his dog, Chloe on his 40th birthday
January 18, 2007

Making foolish business investments with never a concern for their consequences played havoc with his and Sarah's financial situation. Purchasing expensive items he'd never use and making large donations to people and organizations became costly.

Requiring little to no sleep, while operating a motor vehicle, he was an accident waiting to happen. Driving at high speeds with reflexes slowed from lack of sleep not only put him at risk, but endangered all the other innocent people on the highway with him.

His ability to beat the system was frightening. When manic, he possessed an uncanny ability to outsmart doctors, judges, crisis control units, and the police. The more he practiced, the better he got, and the system gave him plenty of practice.

It frustrated and angered me that the laws had swung so far in the direction of protecting the rights of the mentally ill. These laws, though well intended, prevent families such as mine from getting their ill relatives treatment. Scotty's illness erased any sign of reality. He never realized he was ill, while the law hamstrung his family; we couldn't get him the treatment he needed in order to rejoin society. Exceptions to this harmful legislation need to be made in severe cases such as Scotty's.

State legislators don't seem to grasp the serious consequences to the patient as well as to society when bipolar disorder is left untreated. According to clinical research and studies, the longer these individuals go untreated, the more difficult it becomes to treat the illness and the more uncertain their prospects for long-term recovery become. These same studies indicate that early treatment produces better clinical outcomes.

When the judge released Scotty following his hearing at Mount Vernon Hospital, Scotty borrowed a car under false pretenses and made his way to Raleigh. Driving at high speed, he could have killed himself and others. Who then becomes liable for the death of innocent people? Scotty, who was very psychotic, and too sick to know that he was sick? The judge who released him? Scotty's family, who knew he was too ill to drive a car, but was unable to get him hospitalized for treatment? Or the mental health care system?

George and I knew we had to do something to protect Scotty from himself. We decided to make an end run around this crippling law and consulted a lawyer who represented mentally ill clients and their families. The lawyer's first order of business was to review the Virginia commitment laws.

"Virginia law requires that your son be found an imminent danger to self or others before he can be forced into treatment," he said.

"Believe me, we're very familiar with this law," I said. I summarized Scotty's three previous episodes and explained our concern that each breakdown was becoming more violent and occurring more frequently. I described our difficulty getting him treated and my family's experience with the Virginia law that he had so eloquently recited.

"The purpose of our visit today is to discuss a legal way around this law," I said. "For instance, George and I each have a living will declaration appointing the other to act on our behalf for the purpose of making health care decisions should we become incapable of making our own. What if my son signs a power of attorney for health care, waives his right to make health care decisions for himself, and delegates this authority to family members?"

"That might work," he replied, "but I've never seen a person with bipolar disorder willing to delegate this authority."

"Right now, he's still recovering from his last breakdown," I said, "but when he gets well again, we'll talk with him. I think he will agree the time has come to be more proactive with his treatment."

"That being the case," the lawyer said, "I'll prepare the document for you."

George and I opted to draft the power of attorney and have the lawyer review it. He made only minor changes to this two-page document, for which he charged a substantial fee.

Scotty and I hassled over the wording of the document for several weeks. He agreed that the power of attorney was necessary, but nevertheless refused to make it irrevocable. He viewed such permanency as a complete loss of his rights, and optimistically believed that his illness might go away someday.

Sarah approved of our efforts. She, like the rest of us, preferred that the power of attorney be irrevocable, but this was a start.

"If only it will be effective at a hearing," she said apprehensively.

"It will be a test case," I assured her. "According to the lawyer, nothing like this has ever been tried, but it just might work."

During one of her evening visits with Scotty, she presented the power of attorney for health care to him as a condition for her return to the marriage. He agreed to sign it, and on December 9, 2002, executed the following agreement.

VIRGINIA DURABLE POWER OF ATTORNEY FOR HEALTH CARE

1) I, Scott C. Baker, residing at _____, am signing this document in the presence of a witness and notary public. I am executing this document to enable my family to help me get treatment when I'm unable to make rational decisions on my own.

2) I have Bipolar Disorder, first diagnosed in 1993, and have had three manic episodes. During each episode, I've refused medication and refused to commit myself voluntarily to a mental hospital for treatment.

3) I realize that my illness, Bipolar Disorder, may prevent me from seeking necessary medical treatment.

4) Accordingly, at such time in the future that a doctor certifies that I am in need of immediate mental health treatment as a result of my mental illness, I waive all my rights to make decisions regarding my healthcare (both physical and mental), and hereby appoint the following individuals to serve as my agents. They (any two of my family members

listed below) are authorized to make all health care decisions on my behalf, including, but not limited to, admission to a mental institution or health care facility.

Sarah Baker, Chris Baker, Jeff Baker, Tricia Cribb, Kathy Holmes, Dorothy Pacharis

5) My agents have full power and authority to make health care decisions for me, including the power to:

    a) Request, receive and review any information, oral or written, regarding my physical or mental health, including, but not limited to, medical and hospital records and consent to disclosure of this information.

    b) Employ and discharge my health care providers.

    c) Authorize my admission to or discharge from (including transfer to another facility) any hospital or medical care facility or program thereof.

My agents do not have the power, under any circumstances, to authorize electroconvulsive therapy (ECT) for me even upon the recommendation of a doctor.

6) By signing below, I indicate that I am emotionally and mentally competent to make this appointment as of this date. I realize that, in the future, when a doctor certifies that I am in need of immediate mental health treatment as a result of mental illness, I may do everything in my power to have this document declared invalid. I hereby request that my protests regarding the authenticity of this document be ignored, and that my agents follow their authority as granted in this Durable Power of Attorney for Health care.

_____   _____

Scott C. Baker   Date

SIGNED and DECLARED by the said SCOTT C. BAKER, being of sound and disposing mind and memory and over the age of Twenty-one (21) years, in my presence, who at his request, and in his presence, have hereunto subscribed my name as attesting witness this _____ day of _____, 2002.

Signature of Witness
Address

COMMONWEALTH   OF   VIRGINIA   COUNTY   OF
_____ to wit:

Subscribed and sworn to before me this _____ day of _____,
2002.

_____, Notary Public
My Commission Expires:_____

With this signed Power of Attorney for Health Care in her possession, Sarah returned to the marriage. She was happy to be home again, with renewed optimism that she would no longer be at the mercy of some judge to make her husband's health care decisions. We all shared her optimism.

Scotty searched for employment once more. After seeing him in action during a manic episode, employers always found a way to terminate him. To prevent any possible lapse in health care insurance during future episodes, Sarah added him to her coverage through her employer. She worked as the catering sales director for a large catering company in Arlington.

It wasn't until spring 2003 that Scotty found employment, this time with an information technology training company doing routine accounting work. He hated the job, didn't work well with his supervisor, and felt stressed. He left after a year and went to work for a mortgage company.

Well aware that stress could be disastrous for someone with bipolar disorder, Sarah concurred with his decision. She worried that the stress of not getting along with his boss might trigger another episode.

Aside from a few isolated incidents of hypomania quickly controlled by Sarah's attentiveness, Scotty continued to do well.

"My biggest fear is the recurrence of another manic episode," he told us many times.

We shared his fear.

One late summer Saturday afternoon, Sarah and Scotty made the hour-and-a-half drive from Oakton to our home in West River for our annual neighborhood block party. They had a good time, and we enjoyed their company. After the party, the four of us watched the sunset from our pier.

Out of the blue, Scotty announced, "Sarah and I are thinking of starting a family. What do you think of that idea, George?"

Although George and I had never discussed children with them, we hoped they would forego parenthood because of Scotty's illness.

Though Scotty's question caught us off guard, George responded without hesitation.

"Scotty, if I had bipolar disorder, I would not have children, because the illness can be hereditary."

Disappointed with George's response, Scotty turned to me. "How do you feel?"

"I agree with George," and I went on to explain, "If I had any illness that was hereditary, I would not take the risk of passing it to my children or grandchildren."

My response increased Scotty's disappointment.

"I know more about bipolar disorder than either of you ever will," he yelled in a disrespectful tone of voice. "If one of my children or grandchildren is ever diagnosed with this illness, I can help him manage it."

This conversation put a damper on what had been, up until then, a very nice day. Angry with us, Scotty wasted no time leaving.

During their ride home, Sarah tried to reason with him.

"Scotty, I'm not so much worried about the heredity aspect of having children. I'm more concerned about how you will handle the stress of children. I want to make sure you're healthy before we start a family, and you have to prove to me that you can manage your illness."

She continued, "How do you think I would feel if you took our child on one of your manic high-speed chases, trying to escape federal agents? You will make a great father, and I don't want bipolar disorder to prevent you from being one. However, you have to stay healthy, you have to take care of yourself, and you must prove to me that you can do all these things before we start a family."

Sarah later shared with me that what really upset Scotty was his impression that George and I implied he should never have been born because his biological mother was bipolar. Of course, we had meant no such thing.

Over the years, Scotty often referred to his mother as bipolar, though she was never diagnosed with bipolar disorder. Her diagnosis was "severe depression disorder," and she suffered from alcoholism, as well.

"No one has perfect genes," Sarah told me, further explaining her position on children, "and it's impossible to prevent anything negative from being passed down from generation to generation. I know the statistics are against him, but I want Scotty to live a normal life that includes fatherhood if he can prove to me he's in control of his illness."

Sarah's feelings about Scotty becoming a father enhanced the admiration I already felt for her. What an amazing woman. He was so fortunate to have her in his life.

Angry with me, Scotty distanced himself for several weeks before calling.

"Do you two have any idea how long it has taken me to convince Sarah to have children with me? In a matter of minutes, you and George blew my chances with your negative response."

"Scotty," I explained, "I appreciate how badly you want to be a father. Even so, I stand by my concerns that bipolar disorder can be hereditary, and I think it's selfish of you to risk passing this gene to your children."

Scotty's anger eventually subsided, but he never forgave us for expressing our opinions in front of Sarah. Some of Scotty's siblings disagreed with us, and encouraged Sarah and Scotty to start a family if that was what they both wanted. These two were getting parenthood advice from all sides.

Several months later, Scotty called late one evening.

"I want to buy your condo in Fort Myers Beach. I'll pay cash for it," he assured me as if he had unlimited funds. Quickly moving to his next thought, "I've started a couple of secret companies, but can't tell you about them. They're secret," he said in a hushed tone of voice.

Recalling his prolonged wrath in the aftermath of our parenthood conversation, I made no attempt to challenge him. I didn't even suggest he get his lithium level checked. Instead, I spent a sleepless night praying that his phone call was a false alarm. That same night, he went to Chris's house, rang the doorbell, and hid behind the bushes. Ringing the doorbell a third time, he jumped out yelling and screaming when Chris opened the door. Upon learning this, I knew his behavior was not a false alarm.

I contacted Sarah. She, too, was concerned.

"With Scotty," she explained, "I try to be very careful not to overreact and distinguish between his sense of humor and warning signs, but he's not sleeping and that worries me. My sister spent some time with him recently, and she shares my concerns."

That evening, Sarah told Scotty that she and a family member were concerned he was becoming ill again. She accompanied him to the doctor the following morning.

A blood test revealed no signs of mania. Surprisingly, the blood test indicated that his lithium level was nearly toxic, prompting the doctor to adjust his medication.

Looking back, I realize the toxic lithium level had resulted from Scotty's over-medicating himself prior to his blood test. That enabled him to achieve a false reading and prove to Sarah and me he was not getting ill again. Over-medicating could have produced a life-threatening situation for Scotty. In addition, the doctor's decision to reduce his lithium dosage, based upon a false reading, could have brought on another manic episode.

Through the process of elimination, Scotty soon discovered that I was the one who'd called Sarah. His anger level reached a new all-time high, completely out of control. I was, for the first time, frightened of him.

"So, you're the one who reported me!" he yelled. "Why don't you just mind your own goddamn business, stay the fuck out of mine, and don't ever communicate with me or my wife again," he screamed, slamming down the phone.

He hung up before I could respond, "But Scotty, your mental health is my business. Please don't be angry with me… I'm trying to help you."

Unkind and downright nasty "Scotty messages" filled our answering machine for several days. I deleted his disrespectful emails without reading them. The degree of his anger was so disconcerting that, this time, I distanced myself. I needed a "Scotty break."

Months passed. Family members updated me, but Scotty and I had no communication. Hurt, I held out for an apology that never came. Then one day, Scotty emailed the following poem he wrote recalling childhood memories and told me he missed communicating with me.

George Pacharis
_____

From: Scott Baker [scottbakercpa@hotmail.com]
Sent: Tuesday, February 03, 2004 4:08 PM
To:
Subject: Remember When?

Remember when I was a young lad and when it was my turn to say grace before dinner? I would say some long ones and the food would get cold. Remember those days?

Remember when I would referee soccer games and then come in from the cold to that awesome chili dinner with corn bread?

Remember when you had to keep my door shut because my room was neater than the rest of the house?

Remember when Chris broke off his toe nail when the sewer lid fell?

Remember when Jodi put the entire mini-bar in her suitcase at the Homestead and thought it was free?

Remember when Tricia drank and danced at your 60th birthday party?

Remember when Baker had puppies? And then had two more the next day?

Remember when I would call from the nurses office so I could go to Burke Lake and you would let me go?

Remember Lorie Kirby? She says hello. She lives in Columbia SC and we talk once a week on the phone. Sweet girl.

Remember when Chris used to tease Jodi about rubbing Ernest's shiny little head?

Remember when the front desk called to ruin the surprise party?

Remember when we would email sometimes and keep in touch?

Remember when we would smile when we got an email from the other one?

Remember when the sun shined bright, the sky was blue? Well, I miss communicating with you.

Remember when that big fat girl took my donuts and threw them down the sewer and I think you had to speak to her? We called her ten ton Tilly.

Remember When   brought to you by Scott Baker.

The poem was Scotty's indirect way of apologizing. It had become difficult for him to say, "I'm sorry."

We all felt his wrath, but made allowances for his behavior. We loved him — good days and bad. Mental illness was not his fault. Each episode robbed us of this kind, gentle human being whose infectious zest for living each day to the fullest touched us all. How we hated this illness and our inability to help him.

10. RAGE, REVERENCE, AND THE RIGHT TO BEAR ARMS

Soon after celebrating their fourth wedding anniversary in March 2005, Sarah spotted troublesome signs of elevation and suggested Scotty check his levels. Calling for an appointment, Scotty learned that his psychiatrist had died of a heart attack, news that devastated him. He had a wonderful working relationship with this doctor and considered him a friend.

We were sorry for the doctor's family, but as selfish as it seems, we were more concerned that Scotty might suffer another manic episode. And we were right. We watched with horror as this sudden death quickly took its toll on Scotty. Signs of elevation worsened. He began staying up late at night and not sleeping — a Code Red alert demanding medical attention.

"Please," Sarah pleaded. "Come to bed and get some sleep."

"I can't sleep," he said. "Don't worry. I'm just watching television, trying to relax."

One such night, he heard noises and thought a raccoon was in the attic. Determined to catch it, Scotty went into the attic, fell through the ceiling above the guest bedroom, and left a large hole in the ceiling. He caught himself before falling to the floor.

He went to a starving artist art sale and purchased a large ugly painting. It was completely out of character for Scotty to frequent an art sale, much less purchase art.

Several days later, without even discussing paint colors with Sarah, he hired a painter to paint the interior of their house.

Sarah's frantic early morning phone call to Chris said it all.

"Scotty is full-blown manic again," she told him tearfully. "He has slept very little during the last four days. He told me to leave, because I'm not a strong enough Christian for him. I'm back at my parents' house trying to locate a new doctor for him."

Poor Sarah spent the entire day trying to locate a new doctor who would see Scotty immediately. Complicating matters, full-blown mania for Scotty translated into full-blown religious. He would only agree to see a Christian psychiatrist.

The deceased doctor's staff, though sympathizing with Sarah's crisis, offered no assistance in getting another doctor.

Calling one doctor's office after another took time, lots of time. Awkward as it was to ask if the doctor was Christian, Sarah was desperate. With each call, she described the severity of her husband's illness, pleading for help. Never permitted to speak with a doctor, she had to explain the situation to many receptionists.

Most psychiatrists are reluctant to take a new patient in the middle of a manic episode, because they're unfamiliar with the patient's medical history. Every doctor's office instructed Sarah to call the Fairfax County Mobile Crisis Control Center or take Scotty to Mount Vernon Hospital for emergency treatment.

Sarah knew Scotty could easily convince the crisis control center that he was not an "imminent danger to self or others." She also knew that driving Scotty to Mount Vernon Hospital for emergency treatment was not going to happen.

Eventually, she located a Christian clinical psychologist who agreed to meet her and Scotty. He was not a medical doctor or authorized to write prescriptions. It was a long shot, but Sarah hoped he could at least convince Scotty to go to the hospital. He was of no help, and the drive to his office wasted time and effort.

The onset of this breakdown coincided with spring break for Virginia public schools. Tricia's children were out of school for the entire week, and she and her family were in nearby Washington, DC, sightseeing.

When she learned her brother was at his in-laws' house in Springfield and the police had been called, Tricia left her family and drove to their home. The police talked with Scotty, and he left quietly. The police and Scotty were gone by the time Tricia arrived.

After leaving his in-laws' house, Scotty received a ticket for running a red light in Fairfax. Even before Sarah knew about the traffic violation, the new dents in his car told her he'd been driving recklessly.

Later that day, Scotty contacted an employee at the law firm where I had worked.

"I need your help," he pleaded. "My phone is tapped and government agents are watching my every move. I'm calling from a phone booth so they can't hear my conversations."

Sensing Scotty was manic and wired, she thought it best to listen and let him talk.

"I need your email address so I can communicate with you. That is, if the FBI and Secret Service have not completely blocked my email. Also, give my email address and telephone number to the managing partner. Tell him to call me immediately. This is an emergency. People are trying to kill me. I fear for my life. You must help me."

To appease him, she agreed to comply with his requests.

The following day, yelling and preaching in his yard, Scotty was arrested for disorderly conduct. When Scotty resisted arrest, the situation became hostile, prompting the two police officers to call for back-up assistance. Two additional police cars arrived, and Scotty was Tasered twice. Handcuffed, with two Taser wounds in his chest, he was transported to Fairfax Hospital for treatment and then transferred to the psychiatric ward at Mount Vernon Hospital. A hearing was scheduled.

Tricia and Sarah found the house trashed and damaged and made a feeble attempt to establish a semblance of order. The front door would not close; the doorframe had been smashed again. Scotty had completely disassembled the radio "to debug the house." Broken glasses and dishes cluttered the kitchen floor. Empty medicine containers and pills were scattered throughout the house. In the basement, they discovered a shrine to his deceased father, complete with photographs and candles that had been burning.

That evening, they visited Scotty at Mount Vernon Hospital. His wrists were badly bruised from the handcuffs, but the nasty Taser wounds upset them. To see holes in his chest brought them to tears.

So we would be better prepared for our next go-around with Virginia's mental health system, following Scotty's third breakdown I had retained a lawyer with expertise in the state's involuntary commitment laws. The lawyer, highly recommended, agreed to represent our family. He praised our efforts in creating the Virginia Durable Power of Attorney for Health Care and expressed optimism it would work.

When I notified him of the hearing, his response was upsetting.

"Sorry, this is very short notice. I've got a client conflict," he said indignantly.

"Short notice, of course it's short notice," I thought. "The hospital can only hold him 72 hours. You know that!

"Can you recommend another lawyer to help us?" I asked.

"On such short notice, I cannot. I suggest your daughter-in-law take the lead at this hearing," citing the Terri Schiavo case that ruled the spouse has authority to make health care decisions.

"Furthermore," he said, "I think Mrs. Baker, armed with the Power of Attorney for Health Care, can plead her husband's case for involuntary treatment as well as I can. As you know, it all depends on the judge. Keep in mind, however, that if the Power of Attorney for Health Care does not work, the next step and last resort is to consider a guardianship appointment. I'd be happy to discuss this appointment with you at a later date," he said. "Let me know how the hearing goes."

Sarah, Kathy, Tricia, and Chris attended the hearing. Sarah had prepared to take the lead. To everyone's surprise, Scotty immediately took charge of the proceedings.

"Your honor, I'm very sick and need help. I want to commit myself for treatment."

The judge tried to talk Scotty out of his decision. "Mr. Baker, let me remind you, you're entitled to a hearing."

Scotty, always several steps ahead of us when manic, was so certain we would use the Power of Attorney for Health Care to have him involuntarily treated that he opted for voluntary commitment, knowing he could leave the hospital in 48 hours.

Scotty settled into his hospital routine. That meant lots of time on the telephone. One of his calls went to the same employee at my old law firm.

"I'm feeling better," he said, "but I still need your firm to represent me in numerous class action lawsuits. Have your best lawyer call me here at Mount Vernon Hospital as soon as possible. I'm in the psychiatric ward, but don't let that bother you. I'm not sick."

The next day, Sarah met with the doctor and caseworker. The family knew that I kept a detailed journal of Scotty's illness, and I emailed Sarah information on previous episodes and hospital confinements for her meeting. Scotty, being present, saw my email, ripped it out of Sarah's hand, and read it. His verbal outrage along with the information on previous episodes and hospital confinements convinced the doctor that Scotty should remain hospitalized for another five days.

Fearing the power of attorney, Scotty agreed to the additional five days. Sarah suggested I not take Scotty's calls until he calmed down.

Two days later, seeing so little improvement in his condition, Sarah expressed concern to the doctor.

"He still thinks he's a Prophet of God and his calling is the seminary," she told him. "In the past when my husband was getting well, he always apologized for getting sick again, told me how much he loved me, and thanked me for sticking with him. But this time he's guarded in his conversations and seems ill at ease."

"It's going to take time," he assured her. "Be patient."

The doctor had Sarah's cell and her parents' home telephone numbers to call with updates. Unfortunately, he left updates on Sarah and Scotty's home phone. Scotty checked this phone frequently for messages and deleted all the doctor's calls.

Sarah was furious.

"Scotty, if you leave this hospital before the doctor assures me you're ready to be discharged, our marriage is over," she said, laying down the law.

Frustrated by what seemed a hopeless situation, a call from the doctor the next day restored her optimism — just what Sarah needed.

"Wow!" the doctor exclaimed. "I just got around to reading your Virginia Durable Power of Attorney for Health Care. This document gives you full authority to make health care decisions for your husband."

"Music to our ears at long last," I thought. At least this very expensive document worked to our advantage with this doctor, although we knew the real test would come with the judge at a hearing.

The doctor shared his suspicions with Sarah that Scotty had been over-medicating himself prior to blood screenings to eliminate signs of mania, something we all felt certain he'd been doing.

"Over-medicating," the doctor explained, "is extremely dangerous, and an overdose can cause your husband to lapse into a coma," he cautioned Sarah.

Scotty, of course, denied over-medicating himself.

With each passing day, we breathed a sigh of relief when Scotty did not exercise his right to give 48 hours notice and sign himself out. Sarah, still confident that he feared her power of attorney, felt he would remain hospitalized until released by the doctor.

Several days later and much too soon for our comfort level, the hospital released Scotty with the understanding that he would attend a five-day outpatient treatment program at nearby Dominion Hospital. It had always been clear to Sarah when Scotty was well enough to be discharged; this time, she was having difficulty reading Scotty. He remained very guarded.

"I'm concerned my husband is not well enough to be discharged," she confided to the caseworker. "There's no doubt in my mind he's still very ill. We'll be back here again very soon."

Although Scotty complied with the discharge instructions and attended Dominion's outpatient treatment program, his caseworker reported he didn't participate in the discussions and almost always arrived late.

Sarah continued to worry about him.

"I promise you, I'm taking my medicine," he assured her. Yet, the next words out of his mouth were, "My calling is in the ministry." We all knew what that meant. Hell was coming.

Sarah, in need of a "Scotty break," went out of town with a girlfriend for the weekend. Scotty drove to Norfolk to visit his sisters and their families.

"He's as bad as when he first became ill with this episode," Tricia told us after spending Friday night with him.

The note he left on her kitchen table during the night simply said, "Can't sleep, going to the beach to catch the sunrise."

Early Saturday morning, he resurfaced at Kathy's after a sleepless night on the beach.

"Had a police escort all the way to Norfolk," he told her nonchalantly. "What a thrill, Kathy, watching those cars pull over on the side of the road so I could drive through."

For reasons known only to Scotty, he left rather abruptly with no explanation and made the three-hour return trip to his home in Oakton. From there, he called his cousin, Sue, who lives in Harrisonburg, Virginia, with her husband, Mike.

"There are people outside my house watching it," he confided to Mike. "I'm not sure if they're good people. Do you think they're here to hurt me?"

"They're good people," Mike assured him. "No need to worry."

After returning from her much-needed "Scotty break" weekend, Sarah managed to get him to agree to see his new doctor. The office visit confirmed what we all suspected.

"Okay, I haven't taken my medicine since leaving Mount Vernon Hospital," he admitted to Sarah and the doctor. "God told me to flush those damn pills down the toilet. The stuff is poison!"

Next, in a heated exchange with the doctor, Scotty shouted, "I'm not sick and you're fired!" He stormed out of the office.

Sarah located another doctor, but Scotty refused to keep the appointment. This doctor had practice locations in Virginia and Maryland. Since she was only in the Virginia office two days a week, it was difficult to reschedule the appointment.

"Because your husband is so ill," the doctor told Sarah, "you need to find a doctor who can accommodate him seven days a week." Meanwhile, Scotty's psychotic thoughts accelerated.

"Sarah," he said, "got a busy week coming up. I've got an important meeting with President Bush at the Homestead Resort in Hot Springs, Virginia. I'm working closely with him, the FBI, the Secret Service, and the CIA. I faxed the president and told him that former President Clinton should be hung. My car and telephone are bugged. So is our house, so be careful what you say."

And then this... "Sarah, I'm so scared," he said tearfully. "Every day I live in total fear for my life. Do you think when they shoot me, they'll shoot to kill?" he asked.

"I've got access to millions of dollars, Sarah," he exclaimed, "with the power to divert this money to area churches where it's needed.

"Sarah, believe me when I tell you, I don't have bipolar disorder. I've never had bipolar disorder," he yelled.

Coping with a manic Scotty was in itself a full-time job. Sarah was spread thin with so much on her plate, trying to work and take care of her husband. She painfully recalled Scotty's track record of damaging their financial situation during episodes, so she found time to monitor their credit card charges, but she was too late. The spending spree had started. He'd spent more than $800 during his weekend in Norfolk.

Sarah cancelled one credit card in both their names, restricted another to a $1,000 line of credit, and closed their home equity line. She had no control over credit cards in Scotty's name and no way of knowing how many he had.

Off to Virginia Beach he went. While there, the police stopped him for walking down the middle of a downtown street swinging a golf club as though he was on a golf course. He was told to get out of the street, but not detained.

His next stop was the Virginia Beach Conference Center Hotel. When checking in, he handed the registration clerk his car keys, wallet, and cell phone.

"Lock these up for me will you, please," he instructed the clerk. "God wants me to stay here and rest for 72 hours."

After taking a dip in the ocean in street clothes, he called Tricia and asked her to bring him some dry clothing. She purchased some clothing and delivered it.

Just prior to the onset of this episode, Sarah and Scotty had contracted to purchase an investment property in Virginia Beach. Because he was ill again, Sarah no longer felt comfortable going forward with the purchase and contacted the real estate agent.

"My husband is very ill with bipolar disorder," she explained, "and we can't go through with the purchase of the townhouse. His illness is causing him to act erratic, and I suggest you not meet with him."

As a worst-case scenario, Sarah expected to lose their $5,000 deposit. However, the agent, sympathetic to her situation, faxed a release.

Tricia took this release with her when she delivered the clothes to Scotty. She found him on the beach and seized the moment to discuss the investment property.

"Scotty," she said, approaching the matter carefully, "Sarah thinks you should hold off on the Virginia Beach purchase. She spoke with your real estate agent and obtained a release from the sales contract. Sarah signed it and wants you to sign it also," Tricia said, handing him the release.

Snatching the release, Scotty threw it on the beach. His face reddened with anger.

"I told our agent I was hospitalized for heart surgery. Thanks to Sarah, everybody knows I have bipolar disorder," he yelled.

Freaking out in front of beachgoers, he screamed and stomped around, a madman.

Tricia had witnessed his anger many times during episodes, but the look he gave her that day was different. For the first time, she was scared of him.

"If Sarah's parents ever witness the anger I saw today," she thought, "they would never want their daughter to return to her marriage."

Leaving him on the beach to continue his manic rage, she stopped by the manager's office and explained her brother's mental condition.

"Don't hesitate to call the police if he gets out of control," she told the manager, "and then please call me," she said, giving him her cell phone number.

Driving out of the hotel parking lot, she saw Scotty on the beach, on his knees praying, making the sign of the cross on his chest. His demeanor had changed from rage to pitiful reverence. She cried all the way home.

In sharp contrast to the Scotty praying on the beach, manic rage took over later in the evening. He trashed his hotel room. He removed the mattress from the bed and left it upside down on the floor. He ripped a mirror off the wall, and remnants of a fire he started in the bathtub were found. He later told us the room was bugged and he was searching for microphones and wires. The damages were billed to his credit card.

Hotel guests, of course, complained. The manager was relieved when Scotty showed up at the registration desk, collected his personal items, and checked out.

Moving on, he checked into the Cavalier Hotel in Virginia Beach under the name of "John Bush," though the hotel let him use his "Scott C. Baker" credit card for payment.

The next day, he mailed a two-by-three-foot Mother's Day card from Virginia Beach, postmarked May 11, 2005. The return address on the envelope read, "Your Son Scott," and the card was addressed to:

> Dottie Pacharis
> Sailor of the 7 Seas
> (An incorrect street address)
> West River, Maryland

Even with his nearly illegible, shaky handwriting and incorrect street address, the post office delivered the card to my house some three weeks later. The card was signed, "Love You, Scott."

Scotty, always so thoughtful about special occasions, usually brought me a bouquet of my favorite flowers on Mother's Day. This year, so very ill and trapped in his bipolar world, he nonetheless possessed the wherewithal to remember the day. It touched me.

Returning from Virginia Beach, he placed a call to his father-in-law in Springfield.

"I'm on my way to your house," Scotty announced. "Furthermore, you need to know that I now have the right to bear arms, and I have a gun permit. I also have top security clearance at the White House."

Upon hearing of this right to bear arms, Sarah called the police. They responded quickly, but Scotty never showed. Instead, he went to his house and called Sarah.

"While in Virginia Beach," he told her, "I completed a very important task. I was declared sane by the United States government and all my legal rights were restored. One of these rights is my individual right to bear arms," he proclaimed.

"Scotty, do you have a gun?" she asked. He refused to answer. "Do you plan to purchase a weapon?"

"You will know in due time," he replied.

We never did know. No gun surfaced. Perhaps Scotty disposed of it for reasons known only to him, or perhaps for fear that he might use it. Probably, no gun existed.

After Scotty announced that his right to bear arms had been restored and he had a gun permit, Sarah's safety and that of her parents became a real concern. This talk about weapons was something new and totally out of character for Scotty.

The reality is this: My son provides a perfect example of why mentally ill people involuntarily committed to a mental hospital should never be allowed to purchase guns. After his first involuntary confinement in 1994, Scotty's name should have been entered into the FBI's database for gun-purchase background checks. Doing so would not have violated his rights, but it would have protected the rights of innocent people that Scotty may have mistaken for the federal agents he thought were trying to kill him.

Adding to the worry about his right to bear arms and buying a gun, someone found his wallet on a preschool playground. Scotty had no idea how it got there. And then a neighbor complained that Scotty was talking to her young son while the child was alone in his driveway playing basketball.

In the world we live in today, I understood the neighbor's concern for her son's safety. As a mother and grandmother, I appreciated where she was coming from. Scotty just loved being around children. I knew this — the neighbor did not. A devoted uncle to his nieces and nephews, he wanted in the worst way to be a father. He longed for the house with the white picket fence, lots of children rushing to greet him at day's end, and being called "dad."

For years, he was active in Big Brothers of America, organizing fundraising activities and adopting Big Brother style two young boys and mentoring both to adulthood. In my mind's eye, I see Scotty watching the little neighborhood boy playing basketball, wishing he had children of his own.

One thing was constant: His psychotic thoughts continued to rage in many directions.

"I hope the government agents will shoot to kill so I don't have to suffer," he told Tricia. "Do you think they will shoot me in the head?"

His answering machine now said, "Scott Baker Ministries," followed by his version of the Sermon on the Mount.

A neighbor, alarmed by Scotty's unusual behavior, called the police. By the time the police arrived, Scotty was gone. While at the house, the police saw a burning candle on the dining room table and contacted Sarah for permission to extinguish it. Inside, they found three candles burning in the bathroom. Scotty's love of candles, but lack of afterthought in tending them, was a mounting worry and danger.

Later that evening, he was arrested for drunk and disorderly conduct and spent the night in the Fairfax County jail. The drunk and disorderly arrest resulted from his loud, erratic behavior. He was released from jail early the next morning, only to be arrested shortly thereafter, this time for banging on the door of a closed convenience store. Scotty resisted arrest both times, but this second time, the police realized that he was ill and transported him to Mount Vernon Hospital. A hearing was scheduled.

Using her power of attorney, Sarah authorized the doctor at Mount Vernon Hospital to treat Scotty aggressively with a new drug used to control psychotic behavior. We were told that one injection would control his psychotic thoughts for up to two weeks. He was held in seclusion for several days, during which time Sarah was unable to visit him.

On the day of the hearing, Kathy, Tricia, and Sarah came. Upon the lawyer's recommendation, again paid for by the generous taxpayers of the State of Virginia, Scotty revoked his Virginia Durable

Power of Attorney for Health Care. The judge, without reading the document, ruled it inadmissible and freed Scotty.

Kathy, typically a very calm person, became so outraged that she actually approached Scotty's lawyer, got in his face, and yelled.

"I hope you can sleep at night! Suppose he was your brother?"

The arrogant lawyer responded, "Lady, I never have a problem sleeping."

I shared her sentiments. This lawyer knew nothing about the severity of Scotty's illness or his family's efforts to get him treated. His job that day was to get his client released from the hospital. That's just what he did! He got Scotty released, and free again with no ongoing treatment.

Sarah, also outraged, was frustrated beyond words. She had no opportunity to discuss Scotty's previous manic episodes or the psychotic behavior leading up to his latest hospitalization. There was no mention of the neighbor's call to the police to report Scotty's behavior. There was no discussion about his arrest for drunk and disorderly conduct, his subsequent encounter with the police for banging on a convenience store door, nor on the necessity to hold him in seclusion at the hospital prior to the hearing.

"Scotty, listen to me," she said, exasperated. "You leave this hospital, and I'll file for separation."

"Okay," he said in a calm voice, seemingly unaffected by Sarah's threat, and then he quickly left the hearing room.

The following day, the Fairfax County police notified Sarah that her husband's wallet had been found in the parking lot of the United Methodist Church in Springfield, the church he'd attended as a child. When she went to pick up the wallet, she told the police her husband's car was missing. Scotty, convinced his car was bugged, had refused to tell Sarah its location because he didn't want her driving it. The police found the car several days later at a shopping center.

Not having a car was never a deterrent to travel for Scotty. He rented a car and drove to his cousins' house in Harrisonburg.

"I'm very sick and need your help," he told Sue and Mike.

"We'll try to help you, Scotty," they said, and invited him to stay for the night. After they went to bed, he left. His note said, "Going home to see my doctor and Sarah."

At home, after a short nap, he drove two hours back to Harrisonburg, had lunch with Sue, and drove back home to Oakton.

And so the maddening scenario continued. The drives to and fro, the ups and downs, the ins and outs of mania and its rages, delusions, and religious reverence had now been joined by the specter of firearms and burning candles. It all pointed in the direction we feared most.

11. CRUSHED BY A BIPOLAR WORLD

Keeping track of a manic Scotty was not only draining, it was also time consuming, and it would prove crushing. Still, life went on. Chris and his wife had their first child. I was at their home in Virginia helping out when Scotty called, "I want to stop by and meet my new nephew."

Not comfortable having his manic brother around the new baby, Chris gave Scotty an excuse.

"Plenty of time for introductions later. Right now, we're not receiving visitors until our son has all his shots."

To our surprise, Scotty accepted this explanation and made no attempt to stop by. Sarah, however, was invited to see the new baby. Upon seeing her, it was obvious that the weight of the world rested on her shoulders. Scotty's illness had this affect on all of us, but Sarah bore its brunt, a burden that had become unbearable.

She told me she intended to file for divorce.

"It's a difficult decision," she explained, almost apologizing. "I'll always worry about him, but I can no longer live like this."

Her announcement came as no surprise. After Scotty revoked the Power of Attorney for Health Care, Sarah and all of us lost hope of ever getting him treated when he became ill.

"Sarah, I understand," I assured her. "I thank you and appreciate everything you've done for Scotty up until now."

Sarah gave no indication of her timing, but I got the impression she would wait until he was well enough to deal with her news.

Some time later, having had time to take in this distressing but unsurprising news, I asked Sarah about her decision to marry Scotty. I knew she had witnessed the seriousness of his illness early on.

"Did you and Scotty ever discuss bipolar disorder before your engagement?"

"Yes, we did. When we were dating, we talked about his first episode and his belief that it was caused by the drug Floxin, the prescription antibiotic he once took for a urinary tract infection. Scotty thought the episode was just a one-time nightmare. He told me about his many trips to the White House and his hospitalization. He told me his ex-wife was not sympathetic to his illness, and of his disappointment in his father-in-law, who'd encouraged his daughter to file for divorce."

"Sarah, didn't any of this concern you?" I asked.

"You have to remember," she reminded me, "I was only 21 years old when I met Scotty. When he told me he was a little depressed — 'bummed out,' he called it — and was considering taking medication, I thought nothing of it. I knew very little about mental illness, and he seemed okay. He was always lots of fun to be around. I had no reason to doubt that the Floxin caused his first episode."

Still, early indicators had been there all along. Sarah's youth and inexperience with the world made it easy to dismiss Scotty's strange behavior. Hindsight, however, provided a more realistic perspective, though it came late in the game.

"I recall going to movies with Scotty during the middle of the day when he should have been working," Sarah told me. "I was a part-time student and doing waitress work at the time, so my schedule was flexible. He missed a lot of work, but always made excuses. He often slept in, watched a lot of movies on television during the day, and loved to drive around in his truck with no real destination. Even then," she said, "he was taking ministry classes and told me he might become a minister some day.

"I didn't recognize the telltale signs of mental illness," she conceded, "until much later. I attributed his unusual behavior to his outgoing personality. I realize now that he was, even then, very torn in accepting he had bipolar disorder and struggling with taking medication."

Sarah then recalled a conversation after she and Scotty were married. Scotty had admitted that when manic, he pretended to take his medication when she walked into the kitchen at night.

"Knowing what I know now," she said, "this should have been obvious to me, but I never picked up on it."

After Scotty's first episode and his unflinching belief that Floxin had caused his illness, I arranged for him to meet with a product liability lawyer. The lawyer found no evidence to support a product liability claim.

I contacted Ortho-McNeil Pharmaceutical, Floxin's manufacturer, and learned that the drug had been discontinued from time to time and was finally removed from the market in January 2006. Floxin, however, never had any black box warnings, the package insert caution that some prescription drugs may cause serious adverse effects. Nevertheless, Scotty remained convinced that the Floxin he took in the fall of 1993 caused his illness, and perhaps Sarah shared this belief, too.

Life went on. At Chris's house, helping out with my new grandson, I talked frequently with Scotty by phone. Anxious as ever to share his many psychotic thoughts, I did my best to be a good listener.

"God spoke to me this morning from my car radio," he told me with much sincerity. "God has directed me to participate in a volunteer bipolar disorder research program at the National Institutes of Health in Bethesda, Maryland."

"Do you plan to participate?" I asked.

"Mom, you know I always follow God's instructions," he said without hesitation.

"God also instructed me to wear Sarah's bedroom slippers to bring me good luck, but I'm not to call her for 30 days."

Realizing that another lecture about his psychotic thoughts was useless, I asked him if he wanted to get together for lunch.

"That's a great idea. I'd love to do that," he said with enthusiasm.

We planned to meet at one of his favorite restaurants in Centreville.

Chris insisted on going with me. As we pulled into the restaurant parking lot, Scotty stood next to his car. His demeanor was that of an elderly man. His pace was slow; his hands shook. Unshaven, dressed in a dirty T-shirt, sweat pants, and bedroom slippers, my son looked like an elderly homeless person. It broke my heart.

After greeting each other, Scotty lifted the trunk of his Explorer to show off his recent purchases. It was full of Adirondack chairs purchased during a shopping trip to Middleburg, Virginia, earlier in the day.

"They're my welcome home gift for Sarah," he told us proudly. "Do you think she'll like them?" he asked.

"She'll love them," I said.

At a table inside the restaurant, it was apparent that Scotty's severe shaking was going to be an issue. There was no way he could get food from his plate to his mouth or even pick up a glass of water. When the waiter delivered our lunch, I offered to cut the chicken on his plate. He refused. Attempting to do it himself, everything ended up in his lap or flew off the table, embarrassing him, Chris, and me. Everybody in the small restaurant stared. The waiter cleaned up the mess and offered to bring more food, but Scotty declined.

Perhaps most people in the restaurant assumed Scotty had advanced Parkinson's disease, but the shaking was a side effect of antipsychotic medications.

"Scotty, what just happened is not a big deal," I told him. "Don't worry about it."

"Easy for you to say," he replied, quickly changing the subject.

"I miss Sarah. My life would be complete if only she would return," he said tearfully. "I have a prayer routine of 10-minute prayers three times a day. These prayers allow the peace of God to enter my body and heal it. My minister gave them to me and they work."

Scotty's revelation was too much. I went to the ladies' room to compose myself. When I returned, Scotty was confiding in Chris.

"I had terrible diarrhea just before you and Mom arrived and went to the bathroom behind that sign right over there." Scotty pointed to a sign next door to the restaurant. "I used my boxer shorts as toilet paper, so I'm not wearing underwear. I went to the local Hampton Inn to clean up."

He said this without embarrassment, as though it was just as normal as his shopping trip in Middleburg. Later, relating this unfortunate "bathroom experience" to Sarah, he told her "As if the shaking isn't bad enough, now these damn meds are causing me to lose control of my bowels."

Upset with his medications' side effects, we all worried he might stop taking them altogether. Mercifully, Scotty improved over the next few weeks. His shaking lessened until it was only a slight problem. Meanwhile, Scotty and I talked frequently. He was very lonely, so we made arrangements to get together for lunch. I drove to his house in Oakton, where he proudly showed me the home improvement projects he'd performed in anticipation of Sarah's return. Always, the theme of Sarah's coming back underlay much of what Scotty did, much of his hopes and desires.

We had such a nice visit, such a nice lunch. He updated me on his plans to purchase the Virginia Beach townhouse. Even though Sarah refused to purchase this property with him, he felt it was a good investment. It was located close to the beach, and the rental income would almost cover the mortgage payment. He was starting a new job with a mortgage company in Tyson's Corner, near his Oakton neighborhood, a job he felt he could handle and that showed promise for advancement.

"Things are going well, Mom," he said with a big smile. "If only Sarah would return, my life would be complete."

Not wanting to promote false hope, I said, "Hang in there and be patient with Sarah."

I went home convinced that Scotty was completely recovered. I believed he had taken charge of his life again, but Sarah's decision loomed over me. I couldn't shake the anxiety concerning how he would handle Sarah's decision to divorce him. I had long felt that when Sarah could no longer cope with Scotty's illness, real trouble would arrive. She was an amazing woman and had such a wonderful way of motivating Scotty to move on with his life after each breakdown, but everyone has a limit. This bipolar world was crushing not just Scotty, but Sarah, too.

Without Sarah, I feared he would go downhill quickly. How could he move on without his rock?

12. 39 AND DOWN AND OUT

Scotty's 39th birthday was coming on January 18. While it meant another year of hope and heartbreak, it also meant the Virginia Durable Power of Attorney for Health Care would no longer be a viable treatment option. Our last resort was a guardianship appointment.

To have this option in place by year's end would be a relief. We needed a lawyer with expertise in this specialized practice area to help us prepare and secure a guardianship appointment. Several mental health advocacy groups recommended a lawyer in nearby Leesburg, Virginia. In fact, they highly recommended him.

I provided his paralegal with extensive background information on Scotty's struggle. "If your son will consent to the guardianship appointment, it can be accomplished," the paralegal assured me.

My next challenge? Convincing Scotty the appointment was necessary, for I anticipated an uphill battle with him. To my complete surprise, Scotty agreed to the appointment and convinced Sarah to assume the responsibility of guardian. A compelling dynamic had changed the landscape. Scotty would agree to almost anything to preserve his marriage.

Sarah and Scotty met with the lawyer and laid out the history of Scotty's battle with bipolar disorder and the severity of his illness. The lawyer — dashing our hopes — told them he could be of no assistance.

"I've never received a request for a guardianship appointment from someone who presents as sane as you, Mr. Baker," he explained. "Right now, you are of sound mind and body, and no judge will appoint a guardian for someone in your present condition, nor can I say with certainty that this appointment will accomplish what you're trying to achieve when you become ill again."

This lawyer seemed amused by their request... he thought it unique. Why had he agreed to representation in the first place? On his paralegal's recommendation, but not fully informed?

"I'm accustomed to dealing with clients who are very ill," he told Scotty. "You don't fall into that category. I teach classes at George Mason School of Law and think I'll throw this one out there for my students to analyze."

Sarah and Scotty could not believe what they had just heard. Once again, the unfathomable ways of so-called experts dropped the ground from beneath their feet. Sarah and Scotty were prepared to take this final step to make sure Scotty would no longer go untreated, only to be told he wasn't ill enough to qualify, when, of course, he was.

At this point, Sarah lost all hope. After all she had endured with Scotty's illness, this amazing woman had agreed to become his guardian, and all the lawyer did was tell them their request was "unique."

Scotty was angry with me — perhaps, rightfully so.

"You sent us on a wild-goose chase that was a complete waste of time and money... I thought you knew something about guardianship appointments."

Scotty refused to even consider a second opinion. Could I blame him? After working 21 years for a large Washington, DC, law firm where I had admired and respected every lawyer in the firm, I, too, was losing all respect for the legal profession.

Allowing myself a few days to calm down, I called the lawyer's paralegal to remind her of our earlier conversation. She was on an extended leave of absence with an unknown date of return. Was that the truth, or avoidance?

I considered calling the lawyer, but didn't. To this day, I don't believe I could have a civil conversation with this man who found amusement in Scotty's request for a guardianship appointment.

Sarah continued to stay at her parents' house, but visited Scotty daily after work. They did things together on weekends. She, however, made no commitment to return to the marriage.

In August, doctors diagnosed her father with cancer, at which time she decided to remain at her parents' house indefinitely to help care for him. She wanted to spend as much time with her dad as possible, and no longer visited Scotty after work. Instead, she invited him to her parents' house.

Not completely giving up on her marriage, Sarah agreed to undergo marriage counseling with Scotty. They attended approximately ten sessions together. Scotty went several times alone. Although the purpose of the sessions was marriage counseling, the counselor really concentrated on Scotty's health and well-being, while helping Sarah deal with her father's terminal illness. They continued to see each other and spent Thanksgiving, Christmas, and New Year's Eve together.

Scotty's birthday came. We invited him to stay the week with us in Fort Myers Beach in January for a birthday visit. Soon after his arrival, though, George and I quickly realized he was high maintenance.

His sleep pattern took us by surprise. Sleeping until mid-morning, followed by an afternoon nap, was routine. Staying awake most of the night, even though three of his evening medications contained a sleep additive, took some getting used to. His first night with us, I prepared his favorite meal. We watched a movie after dinner and went to bed around 10:30 PM.

Before turning in, George reminded Scotty that our security system was on.

"You can't open any doors without activating the alarm," he warned Scotty.

George never turned on the security system, but we didn't want Scotty leaving the house during the night, roaming around the neighborhood, or frequenting local bars.

Around midnight, Scotty knocked on our bedroom door.

"George, I can't sleep. I'm going out for a few beers. Can you turn off the alarm?"

Unable to discourage Scotty from leaving, George waited up until he returned at 2:30 AM.

The next day, we all went to lunch by boat. After lunch, Scotty asked us to drop him off on the north end of the island.

"I want to do some sightseeing. I'll take the beach trolley home."

The north end of Fort Myers Beach is the island's "party" end. Scotty returned to our house on the south end late in the day, very intoxicated, having hit most of the bars along the way. He went to bed early and stayed in for the night.

Suffering from a bad hangover the following morning, he nevertheless wanted George to take him fishing in the boat. His equilibrium that day was noticeably unstable, a condition no doubt attributable to a combination of hangover and medication. While fishing, Scotty did the unthinkable. He fell off the boat. Fortunately, the water was only four feet deep, so there was no real emergency. Had they been fishing in the Gulf of Mexico, the situation could have been dire.

As we were preparing to turn in that night, Scotty, not yet ready to call it a day, said, "I'm going out to lie in the hammock and watch the stars for a little while. Don't wait up for me. I'll be in later."

Our hammock is located on the dock next to the boat. Concerned that Scotty might fall out of the hammock into the canal, George once again waited up until Scotty grew tired of stargazing and returned to the house.

Scotty loved spending time alone on the beach. He hit all of the hotels' hot tubs. With no qualms about walking right in as though he were a registered guest, he relaxed in their tubs, used their towels, and sunned himself in their lounge chairs.

Scotty was drinking too much beer, but considering his ongoing ordeal, the last thing we wanted to do was treat him like a teenager. He was, after all, a 39-year-old adult. We had invited him down for his birthday so he could enjoy himself and return to Virginia rested and refreshed. Still, he did not act as a responsible adult would. He certainly knew better.

"Do not mix with alcohol" — that warning label was affixed to all his medications and his doctors repeatedly cautioned him about alcohol consumption. One doctor even told him in Sarah's presence, "No drinking; a sip of champagne at your best friend's wedding, and that's it!"

I bit my tongue about his alcohol consumption until his last day with us. As we were preparing to go to the airport, he took two beers from the refrigerator and inhaled them.

"Let me remind you of something, Scotty," I told him, really ticked off after watching him guzzle beer all week. "Alcohol interacts dangerously with your meds, and in addition, it destroys your emotional balance that is so hard to maintain with bipolar," quoting language from a NAMI brochure I had recently read.

"Don't sweat it," he replied in a disrespectful tone of voice, quickly catching himself and apologizing. "Mom, you sound just like Sarah with your lectures! I'm on vacation and don't drink this much at home, I promise you."

Returning to Virginia, he moved back and forth between the houses in Oakton and Virginia Beach, pleading with family members to help him decide where to live. His financial situation was dismal. Struggling with two mortgage payments, he had depleted almost all of his savings. He was living month to month, feeling lonely and depressed.

"Life sucks," he told me over and over again. For sure it did. On all fronts, all he faced was misery.

13. A Pilgrimage into Chaos

The dilemma of where to move was resolved: God spoke to Scotty through his car radio, telling him where to live and more.

"God has instructed me to sell the Oakton house," he told us. "He wants me to move to Virginia Beach and divorce Sarah."

Wasting no time carrying out God's instructions, Scotty put the Oakton house on the market and called his Virginia Beach realtor.

"Don't rent my house when the tenants move out the end of March. I'm moving to Virginia Beach."

Next on his life-changing agenda was dinner with Sarah. He invited her to dinner, and at the restaurant following a lovely evening, he presented her with separation papers. He chose March 3, their anniversary, to serve her.

Sarah went numb, but she wasn't surprised. They had been living apart for almost a year and Scotty was frustrated with the situation. She was already feeling down that day because of her father's illness. He had become too weak to receive chemo, and, in fact, collapsed on the following day, was hospitalized, and was later moved to a hospice.

She was more concerned that Scotty was becoming manic and making irrational decisions than upset about the separation papers. She thought he would change his mind after the episode subsided, but didn't have the energy to deal with it at the time. She had delayed discussing divorce with him, because she didn't feel he could handle it. Looking back, she recalls being a bit relieved that Scotty served the papers and not her. Had she done so, she would have felt tremendous guilt, and Scotty would have believed she was abandoning him.

Making so many life changes at one time concerned us all. Resigning his job, relocating to another city, and filing for divorce in unison would stress anyone out. For someone with bipolar disorder, such changes spelled disaster, an unraveling of life.

March 3, 2001. Scotty picked up the pieces of his life that day when he married Sarah Jordan. Now the pieces lay scattered like a broken puzzle; not one piece fit in the broken life Scotty now had. Fearful, I thought, "This is a catastrophe in the making."

He had a job in Oakton, at least, working at an engineering company doing routine accounting work. While job opportunities in Virginia Beach were bleak, Kathy and Tricia lived in the Virginia Beach area and could provide their brother a wonderful support system.

Scotty's preoccupation with religion convinced Sarah he was elevating again. She urged him to check his lithium levels. Scotty, in complete denial of any elevation, refused to go to the doctor.

"I've started a new company," he told her, "one that sells Bibles and Christian books online." And then, "two trees fell in our back yard yesterday in the shape of a cross while I was praying in the attic. I know this to be a sign from God."

It so happened that George and I were traveling to Virginia to attend a surprise fortieth birthday party for Chris. Thinking we might persuade Scotty to go to the doctor, we tried to get together with him before the party.

"No way," he told us. "I've got commitments to God, and there's no way to work you two into my busy schedule. I'll just see you at the party."

Obviously, he suspected our intent was to lecture him about going to the doctor. I didn't press the issue. Instead, I tried to get him to see us after the party. His response this time was even more hurtful.

"My instructions from God are very clear. I'm to take one day at a time. I don't want to hurt your feelings, Mom, but I prefer to spend my days with God."

Rolling right along, he said, "I'm very stressed out. Sarah and Tricia think I'm getting sick again." Then, "Sarah's father will soon see the face of God, but don't tell Sarah."

At Chris's birthday party, Scotty showed up relaxed and near normal. I breathed a sigh of relief. My comfort level, however, was short-lived. It took only a few minutes to realize Scotty was — beyond doubt — extremely elevated. Although most guests knew Chris's brother was bipolar, I became Scotty's constant companion for the evening trying to keep him away from other guests. His psychotic thoughts were all over the chart that night.

"God is my new boss, best boss in the world," he said proudly. "I'm starting the divinity program at Regent University this summer. I'm already an ordained minister, just need the paper certification from Regent to make it official. I might become a missionary, don't know yet. Do you think I'll make a good missionary?" he asked.

Continuing, "You know, Mom, God does wonderful things for me. I took a bubble bath this afternoon, didn't have to wait for hot water. God supplied it as soon as I turned on the faucet.

"I'm confident I made the right decision to divorce Sarah," he continued. "There's no way I can be married to a woman who refuses to have my children just because I have bipolar disorder. Who does she think she is?"

"You're making a terrible mistake, Scotty. Sarah is the best thing that ever happened to you," I told him. "She's coping with her father's terminal illness right now and really needs your support."

"You know, she might make someone else a good wife, but she's never been religious enough for me," he said. "The only thing I asked her to get me for Christmas last year was a Bible with my name on it. She refused."

Over the years, Scotty's religious mania had been wearing Sarah out. When he'd asked for the Bible with his name engraved on it, her response was curt, "Sorry, no!" She could no longer cope with his religious fervor, tensing up when his religious mania surfaced.

Sarah realized that a very fine line separated Scotty's normal spirituality from mania. Thus, she told him she just would not contribute to anything that might lead to his heightened spirituality. In fairness, she had her reasons. She found it difficult to go to church with him after an episode, because she was much aware of his tendency to become overly spiritual at every episode's onset. His preoccupation with religion literally had her sitting on the edge of her seat with anxiety and apprehension.

Throughout that evening at Chris's house, while most celebrated, Scotty and I talked. He did most of the talking, while I listened with apprehension, as he drank too many beers. It was neither the appropriate place nor the right time to discuss his alcohol consumption, but I was worried about him driving home.

It appeared the party would continue into the night, and George and I had a long drive back to our house in Maryland. Before leaving, I shared my concerns about Scotty's mental condition and alcohol consumption with one of Chris's friends. He assured me he would keep an eye on Scotty and get him home safely.

As it turned out, Scotty left abruptly. Not long after we left, Scotty ran out of the house, yelling.

"Chris, I've got to get out of here!"

Months later, Scotty explained his abrupt departure that night. "It's a perfect example of how bipolar disorder distorts your thoughts," he told me. "I saw all these planes flying over Chris's house. At first, they made me feel safe. I thought they were there to protect me. When I realized they had bombs on board and I was their target, I had to get out of there. Otherwise, I feared everyone at Chris's house would be killed."

Chris's house sits in one of the flight paths for Dulles International Airport. Depending on wind direction, airplanes fly over 24 hours a day, seven days a week.

I called Scotty at home the morning after the party. He was leaving for Sue and Mike's house in Harrisonburg and didn't want to talk.

Sue had done her best to discourage Scotty from making the two-hour drive.

"Mike is very busy right now with tax season, she told him. It's not a good time for a visit."

Not easily discouraged when manic, Scotty drove to Harrisonburg and spent the night with them. He talked a lot about God, assuring them he'd had his lithium levels checked and was fine. He returned to Oakton the next morning.

His next call was to Kathy.

"I'm on my way to your house."

Shortly thereafter, he called Tricia.

"Expect me very late tonight," he said.

Tricia, uncertain whether he would go to Kathy's house or hers, left her door unlocked and went to bed. When manic, Scotty always preferred driving late at night.

When Tricia's husband, Dean, got up early the next morning for work, he found Scotty with a lit candle in their living room doing his devotions. Dean awoke his wife. By the time they returned to the living room, Scotty was on his knees in their six-year-old son's room at the foot of his bed praying. He was asking God to bless his nephew with a nice day.

His next stop was Kathy's school. Kathy, a guidance counselor at a public middle school in Chesapeake, was walking down the hall to the principal's office in the midst of dealing with a problem student. Much to her dismay, she saw Scotty walking toward her. Preoccupied with her student, she could not stop to talk with Scotty, so he proceeded to the school gymnasium and joined a physical education class in calisthenics taught by Kathy's husband, a physical education teacher. When done with his exercises, Scotty left the gym and went to Kathy's office, gave her a hug, and said to the student, "God bless you, young man."

Scotty had never been to Kathy's school before. He did not sign in at the office as visitors are required. Kathy never learned how Scotty managed to get into her school without signing in, roaming the halls without anyone questioning him, but he did.

After leaving Kathy's school, he drove to Regent University, also in Chesapeake. The school was offering a two-day preview seminar for students interested in pursuing a degree in divinity. According to Scotty, "God was calling him." He had previously applied for admission and was awaiting acceptance. The prospect of attending Regent kept him occupied.

A week passed uneventfully. Then he announced an about-face of sorts. "I've decided not to divorce Sarah or sell the Oakton house. I now realize it was my fault all along that Sarah stopped loving me. All this time, I thought it was Sarah who needed to get right with God, when, in fact, I need to focus more on the Lord."

Several days later, I received a long email from Scotty with what he considered an optimistic update on his life. For me, it was depressing.

"I'm taking online classes at Regent University. That way, I can live in both the Oakton and Virginia Beach houses. I don't have to sell either one of them now. I have enough money in my Individual

Retirement Account and stock portfolio to pay my tuition and living expenses." That, of course, was not true.

Scotty's email continued, "I'm setting up a corporation to sell Christian products online and an S Corp called 'God is My Pilot, Ltd.' designed specifically for online Christian store web sites. The S Corp will provide a hefty income based upon my analysis of Spread the Word Ministries. I'm excited about serving the Lord full time. I love Sarah, but must experience grief and cry out to God for help."

His email continued, "I've got to start spending more quality time with Buddy. His alcoholism has accelerated. He's not doing well and needs my help. I'm taking him to St. Croix in the Virgin Islands for a week. We'll spend time praying that God will help him stop drinking."

Scotty's concern about Buddy's alcoholism was based in reality. Over the years, Buddy had developed a serious problem with alcohol. His illness was, unfortunately, exacerbated after Scotty's diagnosis of bipolar disorder. Besides dealing with Scotty's illness, Buddy's drinking worried us.

Scotty's email ended with "Remember, Mom, the best things in life are free, and the greatest of these is love. Don't worry about me. I'm doing good, sleeping well, going to the gym. You'll be proud to hear my weight is down to 214 pounds."

This bit of cheer was misleading. There's an old expression that sums things up. "Things will get worse before they can get better." For Scotty, that saying should have been "Things will get worse and then they will get even worse." Scotty's clouds no longer had any silver linings.

14. Scotty's Story

Driving to upstate New York the next day, Scotty arrived unannounced at the home of his friend, the former owner of the bike shop where he'd worked during high school. After the briefest of visits, Scotty left as abruptly as he had arrived. The visit, however short, accomplished one thing. His friend realized Scotty was very ill. He immediately contacted Sarah to let her know Scotty's location.

Shortly thereafter, Scotty called Kathy.

"I'm in New York on vacation and visiting friends. I'm also looking for a man named Dan who is the director of the National Empowerment Center. Dan is schizophrenic and takes no meds. He has written a book on how to manage life and mental illness through faith in God without medications."

Dan's book inspired Scotty to start writing a book about mental illness. What follows are excerpts from Scotty's effort to write his own book.

Faith Is A Cure For Manic Depression — Together We Can Save Children's Lives And Their Children's

Introduction

My Mom committed suicide when I was eight years old. She tried it several times, and I remember at ages six and seven finding her and calling 911 a couple of times. I found her once in the bathtub with blood everywhere and her wrists slit. Then one time I found her in her favorite comfortable green chair in the living room, out cold with her sleeping pills and other pills all over the place. She always told me, "Scotty, I'm too sick for this world, and I'm going to take my own life. I love you. I'm doing this so that your Dad can find you a good mom to raise you and all you kids can go to college."

In 1975, she succeeded and died of carbon monoxide poisoning when she put a garden hose up to the exhaust pipe, put the hose inside her station wagon and fell asleep forever. A life was gone, a mom gone, a wife gone, a friend dead. She had all the doctors and pills available. But she still died. This method of suicide no longer works, thank God, due to the automobile industry installing mechanisms in the exhaust system to specifically prevent this from occurring.

I asked my Dad years later if there was anything that could have saved my mother. He said "Yes, Scotty there was … if she only had more faith in God, if I had only taken her to church more … she could have saved her life."

Many years later, when I was about 25 years old, I took an antibiotic named Floxin. I felt like Superman, I became "manic." I did all sorts of crazy things and saw all sorts of strange things. I dressed up in my best suit, drove my $65,000 Mercedes Benz company car right up in front of the White House in Washington, DC. I told the U.S. Secret Service agent that I had a message for the president. I told the agent that I envisioned/dreamed that lots of money would be flowing into churches and peace and prosperity would once again descend upon our nation. It was a vision that I had. I was "manic."

Floxin, according to their pharmaceutical insert, causes manic episodes in approximately 1% of the people who take it. Oprah even did a show on Floxin, as it had caused one of her assistants to go to her closet and have a psychotic breakdown. Since this first manic episode, I've had four more. I have seen over 30 psychiatrists and been in approximately eight mental hospitals.

Through grace, through learning the "fruits of the Holy Spirit," I beat this man-made disease of manic depression. For me, I've learned that being manic is simply using a part of the brain that most people don't ever use. More importantly, I have learned that I have a body, mind, spirit, and soul. Thank God, I learned the fruit of the spirit from my dear sister of "self-control."

You see, God did not make any mistakes. Yes, he made some people with diseases, disabilities, and even mental retardation. However, they all still have a body, a mind, a spirit, and a soul. Our current President, George W. Bush, points out consistently that either you are good or you are evil. Everyone has a personality or a kindred spirit. I, by grace and by choice, have the Holy Spirit living inside of me as I do my savior Jesus Christ.

I have learned that, again for me, when I get manic, it is either good or evil. I either want to be rich and famous or I want to be meek and humble and serve the Lord. I ask that you keep an open mind and pray. Pray to God, Allah, or whomever you personally call our one God.

My goal in this book is to offer a cure for manic depression. I am offering a cure for depression, for many of the mental illnesses that imprison your spirit and your children. My Dad was absolutely correct. Faith in God, maker of Heaven and Earth is enough to banish depression.

Faith in God is enough to banish manic depression, and you don't need a $25,000 surgery done to pump Serotonin into your brain as they are now doing. To conclude, it is not the pills, it is not the Lithium, Zyprexa, Haldol, Geodon, nor the Risperdal that cure the mind, body, spirit, and soul. America takes too many pills. They need to get on their knees and pray. Faith can banish depression and manic depression. I promise you with God as my witness.

For The Children

When I was a kid, I did cocaine. I was even addicted to it. One night I had the thought: I wonder what my mother thinks of me doing this. I didn't believe in God at that particular point in my high school senior year. But I remember a youth pastor in Springfield, Virginia, who said "When you really mean it, when you really need God, pray. He will be there." Well, I took my Dads leather Bible out and put it on a chair in our living room and I prayed.

I prayed, "Dear God, oh Jesus, if you're there, please come into my heart, please come into my life and save me from this mess I'm in, this cocaine." You know what? It worked. I went to Straight, Inc. and spoke to a counselor. I saw the 12 steps on the wall, and I leaped right to the one that said believe in a higher power. I have never felt the same since I asked God into my life.

When I was in a mental hospital in Florida, I witnessed little children being strapped down to a bed by their arms and legs. They were given shots of Haldol at the mere ages of about seven to 13 years old. That really ticked me off. So I'm writing this to the Christopher Columbus Foundation and to the National Institutes of Mental Health for Alternative Medicine and to you, not for me, but for the health and welfare of saving our children, as they need help.

America takes more pills than any other nation, I'm told. President George W. Bush said when he was setting up his Faith Based Initiatives Program that he wanted to help heal America. I tell you, simply put: Faith works. Save our kids.

The pharmaceutical industry lobbies the government. The U.S. Food and Drug Administration must approve all drugs for people to take for various mental illnesses. I take Lithium, a drug tested on rats, and nobody knows how it works. I took chemistry in high school and basically when I take Lithium, I am taking a form of salt, which costs $40 a month out of my pocket for 60 pills. I would rather give the money to a faith-based charity. As my former psychiatrist once told me, "Lithium is insufficient for you, and we need to get more medicine in you right away."

My doctor, who was actually a caring man, so I won't defame him, was doing what he thought and believed was right. I was reading the Bible, going to church, caring about my loved ones, and he said I was manic.

The Power Of Prayer

The power of prayer is awesome. How wonderful it is to be able to pray and communicate with our God and creator. He, or She, if you prefer, wants to hear from you and have a personal relationship with you. The Native American Indians have been praying to the Great Spirit for centuries and they do not take as many darn pills as the rest of the Americans.

Pray the prayer that the youth pastor taught me. When you pray, do so earnestly. God is waiting. God wants you to feel better. God is not a pill. I am not saying all pills are bad. Do not misunderstand me. However, when I was strapped down in a four-point hold for singing a Christian hymn and had to literally fight off eight people in the hospital and be shot with Haldol, I was praying. Well, I'm living proof, prayer works. Further, Electronic Convulsive Shock Therapy should be outlawed. I always said, "No thank you."

The Power Of Music

Assuming our great President is correct and you are either good or evil, the power of music can really make a difference in your life. If you listen to good music, it makes you feel good. If you listen to bad music, it can make you feel bad. I change my station when a song like AC/DC's "I'm on the Highway to Hell" comes on, because I don't want to be on the highway to hell. I would prefer to listen to something like Cat Stevens' "Morning Has Broken."

I have experimented and watched several groups of people react to good versus evil music. Listen to the words of the music you and your kids (if God has blessed you with any) hear. There is healing in music and music therapy is important to people.

The Power Of A Shower

A hot shower and a cold shower will change your outlook for the moment. The National Institute of Health– Alternative Medicine [National Center for Complementary and Alternative Medicine] (says we) should focus on the simple things in life, like a shower. We need not spend so much money on pills. I saw a sign once, many years ago, that said, "Psychiatry without God is Satan." I believe this to be true.

Conclusion

To quote a phrase by the Governor of Virginia, "there is another way." There is another way to banish depression. There is another way to parent your children. There is another way to heal mental illness. There is another way to save a soul. There is another way to cure a manic depressive person. There is another way to relieve the stresses that life throws our way. That other way is through faith in God and prayer.

My wife right now thinks I'm ill. She's worried I say "God." She says, "See the doctor." I love my wife, I love my family, I love the Lord, and I love this country. God loves each one of us, Muslims, Christians, Jews, and even non-believers. To conclude, I ask you these final questions. Do you believe we can heal America? Do you believe we can have peace on Earth? Do you care about the little ones? And finally, have you prayed to God lately?

For the children and their children I write this book humbly to the Christopher Columbus Foundation in New York. In the name of the Father, God Almighty, maker of Heaven and Earth and of all that is seen and unseen, in the name of Jesus Christ, my personal savior, in the name of Allah, the Great Spirit, and my personal favorite, the Holy Spirit. Amen.

Rev. Scott Clovis Baker, CPA

President of GOD is My Pilot Ministries

Family Commentary on Scotty's Manuscript

A note concerning Scotty's introduction... Kathy, the eldest of the original Baker children, was 16 when her mother committed suicide. She said that Scotty, age six or seven, may have witnessed the ambulance coming to their house to take their mother to the hospital emergency room, but that he never called 911. He may have found their mother passed out in her favorite green chair from an overdose of pills and alcohol, but Kathy assured me he never found her in the bathtub with her wrists slit.

Their mother's suicide attempts always involved a combination of pills and alcohol, until her successful attempt with carbon monoxide poisoning in 1975. Kathy also confirmed that their mother might have told Scotty she was very depressed and could not struggle with life anymore. She'd said this to Kathy many times.

The pain Scotty was feeling — imagined and real — was sublimated into the pain he came to see in the world's children. It's hard to know what Scotty, at the tender age of eight, perceived as real, but I believe his book's aim was to help others. On his behalf, I hope in this book to continue the work that was going on somewhere in his mind on the run, perhaps to accomplish something that his shortened life kept him from doing — and to help those unable to help themselves for reasons not under their control.

— · —

On the road again, Scotty was driving straight through from New York to Harrisonburg with very little sleep. Then he checked into a hotel and called Sue.

"I've got a draft of my book and want you and Mike to read it."

Though Scotty's demeanor seemed calm, Sue noted he was jumping from subject to subject, struggling to stay composed. She explained they would like to read the book; however, Mike was busy trying to meet some deadlines before they left town and it just wasn't a good time.

"It just wasn't a good time." This thread stitches Scotty's sad story together. It just wasn't a good time to get Scotty enduring help thanks to rigid laws that prevented us from getting Scotty the treatment he desperately needed.

It just wasn't a good time for counselors to see through his self-protective charades.

It wasn't a good time for doctors and bureaucrats to cut through HIPAA red tape.

It just wasn't a good time for esteemed law professors to see how much this young man needed protection from himself, nor was it a good time for judges, blinded by the law, to rule in the family's favor, an insensitive failure that left Scotty vulnerable to the worst outcome of all.

It's heartbreaking to read the story Scotty hoped to share, knowing that a different outcome might have made his message possible. I suppose it just wasn't a good time for Scotty Baker to suffer bipolar disorder — something totally out of his control — unlike the arbitrary rules and situations that counselors, lawyers, and doctors seem to thrive on.

And for Scotty, his family, and Sarah, it just wasn't a good time. Period.

15. SPIRALING DOWNWARD

The next morning, before returning home to Oakton, Scotty left a note at Sue's house on letterhead from the National Empowerment Center.

"I had a nice visit with the Mennonite farmer this morning."

A Mennonite community sits on the outskirts of Harrisonburg.

As Scotty continued his downward spiral, we watched him slip farther and farther away. We could do nothing. The insanity of the mental health system was mind-boggling.

Sarah pleaded with him to go to the doctor. To appease her, and much to our surprise, he agreed.

Because Scotty could still keep it together for short periods, Kathy spoke with his doctor before the appointment to make certain she knew how ill her brother had become. Even without Kathy's call, the doctor immediately recognized that Scotty was extremely ill and recommended hospitalization. Scotty refused, saying he was too busy writing his book. He returned to Harrisonburg for another visit with Sue and Mike.

"I'm in town for a meeting with my publisher to discuss my book," he told them over dinner. "I feel great, and I'm excited about my book."

From Harrisonburg, he drove to Norfolk. Arriving at Tricia's house late in the evening, he jumped on her children's trampoline, rolled toilet paper in the tree in her front yard, and then turned in for the night.

Leaving her house very early the next morning, he took occupancy of his Virginia Beach townhouse. Later that morning, he sent President Bush the following email.

-----Original Message-----
From: Scott Baker [mailto:scottbakercpa@hotmail.com]
Sent: Saturday, April 01, 2006 10:49 AM
To: president@whitehouse.gov
Cc: Sarah Baker
Subject: Thank YOU!!!!!

Dear George,

Thank you so very much for freeing me, for believing in the Lord, for letting the Lord lead you and work through you. You are a Godly man, and I look forward to meeting with you soon. I will be in Texas 4/13-4/20. Want to go to Church on Easter together? I was going to say: know any good fishing spots.

Thank you so very much from the bottom of my humble heart. You make me cry tears; but tears of joy.

God Bless You Richly,

Scott

I am not scared anymore. I feel free. I feel like myself again.
Thanks so much, President Bush. I really do LOVE you, Sir.

The pitiful email to President Bush made us all cry. Scotty, I feared — so far removed from reality, in his own private bipolar world — would never return. This time, more so than ever, I felt the loss of wind in his sails.

We hated bipolar disorder and what it did to Scotty's brain. We hated being unable to get him treatment so he could heal and rejoin society. We hated having to wait until the police picked him up yet again and then start the process all over again with a hearing. How anybody could justify letting Scotty roam the land in this condition and classify it as protecting his rights defied comprehension.

As manic as he was, he played golf with Kathy's husband, John, the following day.

"I'm being escorted by automobiles on the highway and planes in the sky," he confided, while cautioning John, "This information is so confidential that I'm only allowed to discuss it with my immediate family.

"I haven't taken lithium in over three months," Scotty admitted, "and I'm doing just great. I can now purchase life insurance. I'm no longer required to check the box that asks if you have a mental illness," he announced with pride.

Settling into his new Virginia Beach townhouse, he appeared to have not a worry in the world. He was exuberant over having God direct his every move. The recorded message on his telephone said, "You have reached the Rev. Scott C. Baker, and I'm on spring break in Disney World."

And in fact he really was en route to Orlando. He called Sarah along the way.

"I'm aboard the auto train on my way to Disney World," he told Sarah. "My itinerary also includes China and Japan, after a visit with Mom and George in Fort Myers Beach."

Sarah had no way of knowing if Scotty had his passport, but the last thing she wanted was for him to leave the country. She told him we were in Texas visiting friends and begged him to return to Virginia. When the auto train arrived in Sanford, Florida, Scotty got his car, drove to Fort Myers Beach, and checked into a Holiday Inn.

Since we were out of town, Tricia contacted the crisis control center in Fort Myers to help hospitalize Scotty. She provided background information, told them he was seriously ill and needed immediate medical attention.

The crisis control center agreed to send a team to the Holiday Inn, but when the dispatcher passed this information along to the Fort Myers Beach police, they were already familiar with one Scott Baker. He had created a disturbance earlier in the day at a bank. The bank manager called the police, who apprehended Scotty, searched his car, and talked with him. Experienced and skilled, Scotty recited his rights and acknowledged that he was bipolar, was taking his medication, and had everything under control. The police did not detain Scotty. And then he checked out of the Holiday Inn.

From Texas, George checked our home phone messages. Scotty had left four.

"Hey, you two," the first message said. "I'm in Sarasota, being escorted and under heavy guard by the Republican Party; I'm working on impeaching President Bush and the three previous presidents; I have to leave the country for a few weeks to travel to China and Japan; I'm on my way to Fort Myers Beach to spend time with you; I'm exercising my constitutional right to bear arms to protect myself; George, I'm going to need you to teach me how to shoot a gun."

His request to George reminded me of another time when Sarah had asked him if he had a gun, and he said, "You'll know in due time." And so, this talk about guns was not something we could take lightly. It was worrisome.

His second message was just as frightening.

"I fear for my life George; I'm in a bar; call me in the next 10 minutes; I can't stay in any one place longer than 10 minutes without being shot."

The third message was brief.

"I'm at the Holiday Inn. George, call me ASAP."

His last message simply said, "George, please come to Room 144. I'm scared."

On the move again, he left a message for Kathy.

"I miss my dog, and I'm en route to Virginia. I tossed my cell phone but will call when I get home."

Not long after that, Sarah received a call from the Arlington County, Virginia, police. The police played Scotty's message for Sarah.

"My wife is in danger. I request you immediately put a special protection detail on her, because I'm out of town and unable to protect her."

The police told Sarah that her husband had placed this call from a pay phone at an elementary school in South Carolina. He'd signed himself in at the school as the Rev. Scott C. Baker, used the phone, and then left the school grounds.

By this time, Sarah had become immune to Scotty's manic behavior. Nothing he did shocked her. She did not get upset when she talked with the police.

She calmly told them, "I'm fine. My husband is bipolar and off his meds. Just ignore his call."

Later that night, Scotty called Buddy, who now lived in Summerville, South Carolina. Buddy called the police, told them of his brother's mental condition, and requested they pick him up. The police tried to transport Scotty to the hospital, but as usual, he recited his rights and refused to go.

Buddy reached Scotty's Virginia doctor, who spoke to the Charleston County police.

"Scott Baker is my patient," she told the police officer. "He's bipolar, not taking his medication, is very ill, and requires immediate hospitalization."

This wonderful doctor went well beyond the call of duty. Had it not been for her intervention, the police would never have taken Scotty by force to the local emergency room, where he was heavily sedated.

He remained in the emergency room the following day, waiting for a bed to become available in a local mental health facility. Although shackled in a four-point restraint, he managed to flip his bed over during a fit of rage, injuring his wrist. The hospital staff, concerned that his wrist might be broken, did not feel safe taking him to X-ray. Because the hospital was small and had no psychiatrist on staff, Scotty went untreated.

Two days later, he was transferred to the Palmetto Low Country Behavioral Center in nearby Charleston.

"I'll be released in three to four days," he predicted.

Upon our return from Texas, George went to the local bank to get the details of Scotty's encounter with the police while he was in Fort Myers Beach. It was, of course, yet another bizarre bipolar experience.

The bank manager said Scotty had stopped at one of their branch offices in Sarasota en route to Fort Myers Beach, and opened an account with a large sum of cash. He had withdrawn this cash from his credit union account prior to leaving Virginia on the auto train.

After opening the account, he requested a cashier's check payable to himself in the amount of $6,500. He took this check to the bank's Fort Myers Beach branch and asked the teller for $2,500 in cash and told her he wanted to open four business accounts with the remaining $4,000.

Scotty had personal identification, but no business identification. Thus, the bank manager got involved, at which time Scotty grew indignant and called the teller and manager unkind names. At one point during the incident, Scotty did not like a song playing on the bank's radio and smashed it with his fist. He left without opening the accounts or cashing his check. The bank manager called the local police, reported the incident, and described Scotty's car, but the police couldn't locate it.

Later that day, the same teller who waited on Scotty was outside the bank on a cigarette break. Scotty, driving past the bank fast and recklessly with his window down, pointed his hand and finger at her, simulating a hand holding a gun. The teller, fearing she was to become the victim of a drive-by shooting, screamed. The police were called again. This time, they located Scotty and his car. They found no gun and released Scotty because no crime had been committed.

And that's how the Fort Meyers Beach bank incident went, yet another downward turn in this escalating downward spiral that no one could stop.

Checking in with me one night from the Charleston hospital, Scotty talked nonstop. Laughing one minute, crying the next, he rambled on incoherently. His phone call dragged me deeper into despair.

"I've been beaten, injected with drugs, and kept in restraints," he told me, crying. "I don't want you to worry. I'll be released soon and back in Fort Myers Beach, so I can fall off the boat again," he said laughing. "Remind George I still need to learn how to shoot a gun. I'm no longer a Republican. I'm working with the Democrats to impeach George W. Bush. I'm leaving the country in a few days. Don't worry — I'll have an armed escort at all times. I'll be elected president in 2012. First, I'll become a governor in any state of my choice. There is no such thing as Lent. I have three beers a day, one for the Father, one for the Son, and one for the Holy Spirit. I'm proud to call you my Mom, even though you made me eat all the peas on my plate," he said tearfully, abruptly terminating the call. I heard the click, then the dial tone, and he was gone.

"Scotty," I thought. "You're so sick. How grateful I am that at long last, you're in the hospital. I just pray it's not too late to make you well again."

His condition continued unchanged. He was no better, but thankfully, no worse. The hospital was not giving him lithium because he'd overdosed on it right before the police picked him up. His levels were toxic when he was admitted.

Kathy received most of his collect calls. During one such call, Scotty was ranting about Buddy and one of his nurses.

"Buddy doesn't visit me every day," he complained. "I told him to bring me cigarettes, cigars, chewing tobacco, quarters, and telephone calling cards, yet he shows up empty-handed or not at all."

Battling advanced alcoholism, Buddy had his own problems. Having his mentally ill brother hospitalized nearby placed additional stress on him. Moreover, he was trying to work during the day and tend to his family in the evenings.

"That nurse keeps yelling at me to get off the phone," Scotty complained to Kathy. "Why should it matter to her how much I talk on the phone?"

Kathy could hear the nurse in the background telling Scotty over and over to get off the phone.

"I've got to go now," he told Kathy, "but call me right back on this number. I've got something funny to tell you."

When she called the number, a White House operator answered the phone.

The next day, dialing 911 repeatedly, Scotty reported that he was being held hostage. Because the police are required to respond to all 911 calls, the patient telephone in his room had to be removed. He continued to be delusional, and his social worker reported they were seeing no real progress.

One evening, a fellow bipolar patient and Scotty conspired to create havoc in their unit, causing such a disturbance that it was necessary to separate them. Infuriated, Scotty threatened six other patients with bodily harm. The hospital transferred him to the crisis unit.

Another one of Scotty's fellow patients emailed us with instructions to call Scotty's cell phone for an urgent message. Although Scotty had long since tossed his cell phone, he could still change his recorded message and check messages using any phone.

The last thing I wanted to do was call his cell phone and be reminded of just how sick Scotty was. George suggested I ignore the email; I should have taken his advice. Instead, I dialed the number.

"I'm being held against my will in South Carolina. The Charleston County Sheriff's Department had no authority to bring me in. I need your help getting released so I can continue God's work. I do not have bipolar disorder. I've never had bipolar disorder. I'm not sick. I don't belong in a mental hospital. Please help me get out of here before they kill me," he pleaded.

In mid-April, the doctor treating Scotty presented a very bleak prognosis. Buddy was present during the conversation.

"Mr. Baker," he said, "you are the most severe bipolar patient I've ever seen. You are a severely manic-depressed individual."

Scotty, unfazed by the doctor's description, refused all medications. At best, he took a limited dosage, rendering his hospitalization ineffective. Unable to force Scotty to take his medications until after the hearing, and only then if the judge saw fit to write a forced medications order, his doctor was helpless to treat him. Scotty's condition worsened each day. His court hearing was five days away. He threatened everyone in the hospital with citizen's arrest after his release.

Sarah's father lost his battle with cancer during Scotty's South Carolina hospitalization. His death upset Scotty. Although extremely ill, Sarah had a near normal conversation with Scotty that day.

"Is there anything I can do for you, Sarah?"

"Yes," she said, "get better."

Responding in a very calm and normal voice, he said, "I will, I promise."

Because the Charleston County sheriff's department took Scotty to the hospital, Charleston County was responsible for paying for his care at the Palmetto Behavioral Center. The doctor gave Buddy the bad news that county-allotted funds for Scotty's care were running out, at which time he'd be treated as uninsured.

When Scotty resigned from his job in Oakton, he had been given COBRA insurance forms to continue his health insurance coverage, but of course he never completed them. With no health insurance and the money allotted by the county running out, Scotty's name was placed on the waiting list for transfer to a state mental hospital in Columbia, South Carolina.

Having just lost her father the previous day, Sarah had to go to their Oakton house and search for the COBRA paperwork. She found the forms and couriered them to Buddy, enabling the hospital to verify that Scotty was insured before his upcoming court date. He thus avoided transfer to the state hospital in Columbia.

One day, during a conference call with Scotty and the hospital social worker, his Virginia psychiatrist told Scotty she could no longer be his doctor when he returned to Virginia. His illness was simply more than her practice could handle. Scotty, upset because he thought she was firing him, fired her and slammed the phone down.

The day before his hearing, Scotty left two messages on our answering machine. "I'm being released tomorrow and will return to Fort Myers Beach," he assured us in his first message. Two hours later, "I'm still being released, but due to urgent business, must return to Virginia. Catch you two later."

The result of his long-awaited hearing was that Scotty would remain hospitalized until stabile. The judge wrote a 36-month mandatory forced medications order that included regular office visits and treatment if any tests showed that Scotty had gone off his prescribed medications. The order could include automatic hospitalization if necessary, and this judge's order was also enforceable in the state of Virginia. For once, we'd broken through the bureaucratic wall, and it was wonderful news for my family.

The law in South Carolina on involuntary commitment is also less restrictive than the Virginia law specifying commitment if the individual "needs treatment and is either

1) unable to make responsible decisions with respect to treatment; or

2) there is likelihood of serious harm to self/others, including the substantial risk of physical impairment from inability to protect oneself in the community and provisions for protection are unavailable."

After a couple of days of forced meds, we saw some improvement. Scotty would be discharged in four days, provided a family member accompanied him to his Virginia Beach residence. Kathy scrambled to find a new local doctor qualified to treat a patient with severe bipolar disorder, one who would accept Scotty's COBRA insurance.

Buddy met with the doctor, who confirmed that his brother could be discharged in four days provided his lithium level was within the acceptable range.

"Although Scotty is not completely well," the doctor explained, "if he were a South Carolina resident, he would be discharged and enrolled in an outpatient day treatment program. The manic crisis of his illness has subsided to an acceptable level for outpatient treatment, and I can't justify treating Scotty, a Virginia resident, any differently than I would a South Carolina resident."

"I understand," Buddy said, "but based on my visit with him last night, I feel he's at the very critical point of either making a rational decision to stay on his meds or stop taking them altogether. His family wants to put into place the best safeguards possible to prevent Scotty from having another manic episode."

"Sorry, but there will be more episodes," the doctor said. "Your brother's illness has become so severe that to think he can control it on his own will only make it harder on everyone, including Scotty. If your family is looking for safeguards to prevent another breakdown, I'm sorry, there are none. I would, however, like to suggest that based upon your brother's past medical history, your family should have a very strong case for addressing the proper court authorities and being granted whatever legal authority is determined by the court to be best for Scotty."

We had all feared this day. There was a time when Scotty could and did control his illness. Now, however, long stretches of going untreated had taken their toll. Now he was incapable of controlling bipolar disorder on his own.

We were thankful when the doctor agreed to hospitalize him for another four days. Still, Buddy remained concerned. Scotty was getting better, but still had a long way to go. As he was, he couldn't function in the outside world.

A few days later, however, thanks to forced meds, Buddy saw positive signs of improvement. Scotty could sit and talk without pacing. He no longer talked about being a minister, forming new companies, or writing a book on bipolar disorder. Then, just as a hint of hope surfaced, Scotty announced he had no intention of following the doctor's discharge orders to attend an outpatient day treatment program.

"I've just spent 21 days in the hospital," he said, "and this day treatment stuff is just not going to happen."

He agreed, however, to take his medications and see the doctor in Virginia Beach that Kathy had found.

Once Scotty learned his discharge date, he called Sarah to ask that all-important question, "Sarah, is there any possibility we can get back together?"

Not wanting to give him false hope, she was straightforward, "Because you once again stopped taking your medication and did not take care of yourself as you promised, our marriage is over."

It was not the response he had hoped for. He responded softly... "Okay."

Scotty's drug use concerned Buddy. Throughout Scotty's confinement, he repeatedly asked Buddy to get him marijuana. Buddy suspected Scotty's intended use was self-medication. Surmising that his brother had been playing this marijuana game off and on for several years, he discussed it with the doctor. The doctor confirmed that if this was what Scotty had been doing, he might have started the process of training his brain to start rapid cycling. This meant Scotty could be hypomanic, fully manic, or depressed all within a short period, again and again, and the changes could be very sudden.

Marijuana aside, the plan was for Buddy to pick his brother up when discharged. Confident that he could keep Scotty at his apartment for the night, he felt certain Scotty would take off the next day against the doctor's orders. Provided Scotty cooperated, Buddy's plan was to drive him to Richmond the following day, meet Kathy and Tricia for the exchange, and return to Charleston on the train.

The magnitude of this breakdown had taken a heavy toll on us all. Kathy would tell him he was no longer welcome at her house if he got off his meds. She just could not endure another manic episode that was preventable and felt this one had caused far too much hardship on everyone.

Scotty's need for a guardianship appointment pressed harder upon us. We had to build a safety net around Scotty, protect him and his assets, and take charge of his health care decisions. With every episode, we observed his heartbreaking erosion as the illness further damaged his brain and the prospects for full recovery diminished.

Tricia contacted the Virginia Beach chapter of the National Alliance on Mental Illness. NAMI recommended a lawyer with expertise in the guardianship practice area, and she scheduled an appointment.

For all of us, Scotty's discharge date came much too quickly. Just a few days earlier, Scotty's social worker had lectured him on the severity of his illness and the likelihood of being unable to control it without the help of others.

"You must learn to rely more on your family for help," she stressed, "otherwise, the negative consequences can be fatal for you and others."

Her words provided an ominous warning.

Anxious to leave the hospital, Scotty waited in the lobby for Buddy to pick him up after work. After a stop at the drugstore for prescription refills, they had dinner and spent the evening talking.

Early the following morning, he awakened Buddy, "I'm leaving for Oakton."

Unable to talk him out of it, Buddy did get a commitment that he would get in touch with a family member if he had any problems.

"I think he's headed in the right direction," Buddy told us, "and this is not the time to jump on him about taking his medications," he cautioned. "I agree with the plan to meet with the lawyer and proceed with the guardianship appointment, but suggest we wait until Scotty has completely recovered before discussing it with him."

His brother's fifth manic episode had taken a real toll on Buddy. He was struggling. Coping with advanced alcoholism, he had been forced to take the lead for the family on this episode after Scotty made his way to the Charleston area.

We were proud of Buddy throughout Scotty's confinement. He had admirably assumed sole responsibility for dealing with the police, the judge at the hearing, his brother's doctor, and the caseworker. He had done his best, while fighting his own demons, to halt Scotty's downward spiral.

16. LONELY STRUGGLE

The lonely 525-mile drive from Charleston back to Oakton left Scotty exhausted. Throughout the drive, his thoughts drifted toward the toll this illness had taken on his personal life and career. Dejected by the time he arrived home, he did his best to be optimistic about the future.

"I must move forward with my life and deal with everything slowly," he said as though he was trying to convince himself.

Life without Sarah weighed heavily on his mind.

"She was my rock after every episode," he told us tearfully. "Now, I'm on my own. I know our marriage is over; it's just hard to accept. She promised we'd remain friends. I've even been invited to her mother's house tonight for dinner," he said with dread.

"You have a very loving family, Scotty," I reminded him, "one who will always be there for you. Just move slowly as you deal with major changes in your life, and let your family be your rock."

Three days later, he returned to Virginia Beach. Spending time with Sarah proved too painful. His sisters and their families spent the evening with him. Upset, shaky, and embarrassed that he was so shaky, he was still emotional about Sarah. He knew that trembling was a side effect of his antipsychotic meds, and we were worried that he might stop taking them altogether, if he hadn't already.

During previous episodes, in addition to taking lithium, a maintenance drug to help reduce the duration, intensity, and frequency of manic episodes, Scotty also took additional antipsychotic drugs while hospitalized, and afterwards until his doctor felt it was safe to discontinue them. This time, however, in addition to lithium, he was instructed to remain on the antipsychotic drugs indefinitely.

By noon the next day, when Tricia and her husband, Dean, met him for lunch, the shaking had progressed from embarrassing to severe. It not only prevented him from getting food from his plate to his mouth, it interfered with every moment of his day. Nights brought no relief; his out-of-control head shook so badly, he couldn't sleep. In addition to coping day and night with this debilitating shaking, financial worries plagued him. Creditors harassed him relentlessly.

"I just received a bill from the hospital in Charleston," he told Tricia and Dean. "I owe them over $12,000."

Desperate for relief from the shaking, he asked his 21-year-old nephew to get him some marijuana. His nephew refused and reported the incident to his mother, Kathy. She felt certain Scotty intended to use the drug to alleviate the shaking and stress.

Sarah confirmed his marijuana use throughout their marriage. When she first confronted him, he assured her he did it to relax. One of her stipulations for returning to the marriage after his third episode was no more marijuana.

"If you ever do it again, I will absolutely divorce you," she warned him, though she suspected he continued to self-medicate.

He did, discretely, and that revelation wasn't surprising. Substance abuse runs rife among bipolar patients. According to NAMI, "the use of drugs and alcohol adds an enormous and dangerous risk factor to bipolar illness, leading to more frequent relapse, increased suicide attempts, and death."

Scotty's shaking intensified. Desperate, he took matters into his own hands and convinced a former doctor to call in a 30-day supply of a prescription drug that had previously helped control his shaking. Within hours after taking the medication, the shaking lessened.

Restless, he returned to Oakton the following day to get a duplicate Virginia driver's license to replace the one he'd lost somewhere during the most recent episode. His real purpose, however, was to see Sarah.

While Scotty was hospitalized, a private memorial service had been held for his father-in-law, but the public service and burial were delayed due to scheduling problems. Her father had really loved Scotty. As the burial date approached, Sarah felt comfortable inviting Scotty to join her family for the service. He was on his best behavior that day, and Sarah appreciated having his support.

The long-awaited meeting with the Virginia Beach lawyer to discuss a guardianship appointment arrived. Kathy and Tricia had agreed to share guardian responsibility for their brother, and both met with the lawyer. Surprised that the Virginia Durable Power of Attorney for Health Care had not worked, the lawyer confirmed that guardianship was the next step toward getting Scotty treated involuntarily when ill.

"Nothing is foolproof," she cautioned. "It all depends on the judge, the attorneys, the state, and even the city where the hearings are held. If you two are appointed guardian, you will have authority to have your brother picked up by showing the appointment to the police officer or magistrate. There are, however, no guarantees that the hospital will keep him if he's not declared a danger to himself or others."

Explaining further, she said, "The best time to obtain a guardianship appointment is when he's very ill. However, given his medical history, if he were to consent to the appointment when well, I think it would be granted." (This information contradicted what the Leesburg attorney had told Sarah and Scotty in July 2005, a contradiction demonstrating the lack of social/legal consciousness about mental illness and the law in this region.) Although Scotty was willing to give Sarah this authority to save his marriage, Kathy and Tricia felt it unlikely that he would appoint them his guardians.

"Guardianship is a lifetime appointment," the attorney explained, "and if you both predecease your brother, a replacement will be appointed by the court. The appointment can be enforced in any state, and allows the guardians access to all medical records, with authority to make all medical decisions."

A huge drawback to guardianship is the loss of one's driver's license. This stipulation particularly troubled Kathy and Tricia, who felt that a stable, non-manic Scotty needed his independence and mobility.

The lawyer suggested they might consider a mental health conservatorship in addition to the guardianship.

"This appointment," she explained, "grants authority for an individual to handle the financial matters of a seriously mentally ill person."

Neither Kathy nor Tricia felt qualified to manage Scotty's assets and finances, but knew they had no choice but to proceed with the guardianship appointment. The plan was to wait until Scotty was well enough to discuss it.

In late May, George and I persuaded Scotty to spend a couple of days with us in West River. He talked openly about his recent episode, describing it as the worst ever.

"Do you two have any idea how awful it is to actually believe federal agents are trying to kill you? I lived in fear of my life for weeks on end, with no one to turn to for help. George, why do you think I asked you to teach me how to shoot a gun? I had to protect myself."

He told us about calling the Anonymous Hotline Number for Whistleblowers to report he had conclusive proof that Vince Foster did not commit suicide, but instead had been murdered.

Vince Foster was the Deputy White House Counsel for President Clinton. Early in Bill Clinton's first term, Foster allegedly committed suicide, and his body was found in a federal park in Virginia. An investigation concluded that he'd committed suicide, although speculation by some held that his death was a murder plot covered up by the Clintons.

"Right after my whistleblower's call, in the psychotic bipolar world in which I was living, I actually believed the Clinton people were all over me," said Scotty. "There were times when I was never certain whether the people following me were Clinton people or federal agents from the Bush administration."

Scotty's mania had an all-to-common euphoric side, too.

"I can't even begin to describe how awesome it feels to actually believe I was to become the next president of the United States," he exclaimed. "It was exhilarating beyond words. So many things happened this time that I can't even tell you about. If I did, it would scare the hell out of you, and I don't want to do that.

"I hate this illness," he said with anger. "I hate living in fear of another manic episode. This one really did some damage. My short-term memory is now shot. Sometimes, I can't even remember what I did yesterday. I've been robbed of all my self-esteem and self-confidence. Can you imagine me, Scott Baker, without self-confidence?"

Very emotional, he described how difficult his life would be without Sarah.

"She still loves me. I know she does. She just can't endure another episode. Can you blame her? She has always been my biggest cheerleader, and I'm not sure I can get through the aftermath of another episode without her."

Feeling extreme pressure to find work so he could start paying his creditors, who were relentlessly hounding him, his plan was to return to Virginia Beach and meet with a headhunter.

"I regret purchasing that damn Virginia Beach townhouse in the worst way," he told us. "Now, I'm stuck with it until the housing market improves and I can unload it. It's just another one of those stupid things I do when manic. Now, I have two mortgages and no job. How dumb is that?"

Although the Oakton house was for sale, the northern Virginia housing market was in the same slump as the rest of the country. Few prospective buyers even looked at Scotty's house, and job opportunities in Virginia Beach? They never materialized.

"Your employment record of seven jobs during the last ten years is a real deterrent," the headhunter explained. "Prospective employers consider you a job-hopper. Sorry, I have no clients willing to take a chance on you."

Using the Internet, Scotty found a few job opportunities that led to interviews. One interview eventually resulted in a job offer, which he accepted without hesitation. He spent the first week of the new job with his boss in South Carolina. After two weeks, bad news. "This is not working out. We have to let you go."

Taking Scotty under their wing, Kathy, Tricia, and their families did their best to console him. He was lonely; he was struggling. Tricia had him over for dinner almost every night and included him in most of her family activities.

In late July, Buddy visited his sisters and Scotty in Norfolk. Near the end of the visit, Scotty's siblings met with him for a private conversation to discuss the guardianship appointment. Reluctantly, Tricia agreed to take the lead in this discussion. She was very nervous and worried about Scotty's reaction.

"Scotty, she said, "this is a very difficult conversation for me. After every manic episode, we never discuss it, because we know you're embarrassed; you just want to put it behind you and pretend it never happened. However, after your recent illness, we agreed we cannot go through another prolonged episode while you refuse treatment. Kathy and I have looked into a guardianship appointment for you."

Having gotten this far without breaking down, she found the courage to continue.

"Contrary to what the lawyer in Leesburg told you and Sarah, we've been assured by a local lawyer that based on your medical history and the severity of your illness, Kathy and I can be appointed your guardian. When you feel yourself elevating, as good as it may feel to be hypomanic, you've got to get to the doctor. During this phase, we all know time is of the essence. When you refuse, as you always do, we will use the guardianship appointment to have you involuntarily treated."

Choosing her words carefully, she continued, "Please try to understand where we're coming from. A breakdown is far worse on you, but you have to realize, it affects everyone in the family. It turns our lives upside down for months. People live with bipolar disorder, but they must get medical help before they become too manic. You know better than anyone that there's only a short period of time before your mind crosses over into the manic phase, and then it takes hospitalization to get you back.

"We love you, Scotty," she assured him. "We want to help you when you're ill. We will only use the appointment to get you treated, with no jurisdiction over your finances."

The look on Scotty's face said it all. Opposition was immediate and emphatic.

"Let me make it very clear to all of you: You're not going to take away my rights and control me. This is my illness, and I'll take care of myself."

Although emotional from Scotty's harsh words, Tricia nevertheless persevered and put her brother on notice.

"Scotty, if you don't agree to this appointment when you're well, the next time you become ill, Kathy and I will take the necessary legal steps to be appointed your guardian."

Throughout the remainder of the summer and into the fall, Scotty struggled with loneliness, unemployment, and a dismal financial situation. I visited him in early November. It was my first time seeing his Virginia Beach house, and he went out of his way to be most hospitable.

Having been unemployed for most of the year and saddled with two mortgage payments, he was in debt and living off credit cards.

"I just sold enough stock to carry me through the end of January," he confided, "but my investment portfolio is almost depleted."

Depressed not only by his financial crisis, loneliness was taking its toll. His only friends in the Virginia Beach area were his two sisters, their families, and his dog. His dog, Chloe, was a German Shepherd-Collie mix he and Sarah had adopted early in their marriage. Sarah let Scotty keep Chloe for company.

When not with one of his sisters or their families, he and Chloe stayed home or he drank alone at a neighborhood bar. He never read the newspaper, never watched television, never listened to the radio. He had no idea what was going on in the outside world and, furthermore, he didn't care.

I urged him to escape this solitary life and meet new people, but my pleas fell on deaf ears. He joined a gym, but never went to work out. He refused to attend church. Volunteer work held no interest for him any more. I tried to convince him to join one of the NAMI bipolar support groups. He refused.

His chances of working in the accounting field appeared nil. I tried to persuade him to take a job at Home Depot or Lowe's — anywhere that would get him out of the house and provide some income. Though half a loaf is better than none, he considered these jobs demeaning.

Scotty walled himself off from life itself. He left his house every day for lunch, but always ate alone. When not invited by one of his sisters, dinner was eaten alone at the local restaurant/bar. Fortunately, Chloe had to be walked several times a day, which at least got him out of the house for fresh air and a little exercise. He spent a lot of time sleeping and was neglecting his personal hygiene. A daily shower was not high on his priority list.

An opportunity performing routine accounting work at a nursing home opened up in early December, and he gratefully accepted the position. Three days later, the monkey jumped on his back yet again. Dreaded words: "It's not working out." Undoubtedly, his employer felt compassion for him, offering to let him work until the end of the year.

Concern about Scotty's depressing life festered within all of us. While visiting Tricia one morning in mid-January 2007, she talked with him about his life in general.

"Scotty," she said, "I know you're depressed about your job situation and battling loneliness, but let me remind you that our family continues to carry the baggage of our mother's suicide, and suicide is not an option for you." Tearful after getting these words out of her mouth, she managed to say, "Scotty, we're all in this together, and your family will always be there for you."

"Please don't cry, Tricia," he said, giving her one of his big bear hugs, trying to console her. Later, she would recall that Scotty never agreed or disagreed with her that day about suicide not being an option. He just gave her one of his affectionate "Scotty hugs," as if to say, it's going to be okay, Tricia, don't worry.

17. FAREWELL

You know you can't hold me forever
I didn't sign up with you
I'm not a present for your friends to open
This boy's too young to be singing the blues

"Goodbye Yellow Brick Road"
— Elton John & Bernie Taupin

January 18, 2007. Scotty spent his 40th birthday with his two sisters and their families. He had been dreading this birthday because nothing in his life was going well. To be truthful, he'd have preferred to skip it. His sisters, nevertheless, insisted on a festive celebration. Everyone did their best to make it special: Tricia prepared his favorite meal, Kathy baked his favorite cake. They gave him fun gifts and took a lot of photos.

He called me in late January to wish me a happy birthday. Although not on top of the world, neither did he sound low during our conversation. He even sent me a humorous card with a thoughtful handwritten note.

On Saturday, February 3, Scotty took some shirts to the laundry. He was invited to a Super Bowl party at Kathy's house the next day, but decided to watch the game at the local bar since it would be ending so late. Buddy spoke with him during the Super Bowl. He seemed fine.

Sarah and Scotty remained good friends and made it a practice to talk by phone every day around noon. Monday, February 5, she couldn't reach him. Calling throughout the afternoon and evening but getting no answer, she worried and called Tricia, who hadn't heard from Scotty either.

On Tuesday morning, February 6, Sarah, still unable to reach him, telephoned Tricia, who called his part-time job. He was not there, nor had he reported for work Monday. She called Dean at his office and asked him to go with her to Scotty's house.

When they arrived at Scotty's house, his car was not in the driveway, its usual place. The garage door was closed. Going inside, Dean found Scotty's car in the garage. Scotty's body lay in the backseat. Some 32 years after Scotty's mother ended her life with carbon monoxide poisoning, Scotty left this world the same way. He left no note.

The police estimated he had been dead about 24 hours. The autopsy report showed carbon monoxide poisoning to be the official cause of death. The police found empty medicine containers in his bathroom. Their toxicology report revealed no evidence of an overdose.

Scotty absolutely hated taking so many medications to control his illness. I like to think that after he decided to end his life, he took pleasure in flushing the remaining pills down the toilet.

Tricia found his dog, Chloe, locked in a guest bedroom, where Scotty had left her with plenty of food and water. Chloe had become his best friend, and I can only imagine the tearful good-bye Scotty had with her before going to the garage. Chloe now lives with Sarah.

I had long feared a violent death for Scotty during one of his manic episodes. I envisioned a horrible automobile accident during a high-speed chase, with Scotty trying to escape federal agents that he imagined were trying to kill him.

After developing a gun fixation and repeatedly asking George to teach him how to shoot, I feared he might kill people he mistook for federal agents. He never got a gun. Scotty just went to sleep and died peacefully... I pray.

I'm so grateful he never hurt anyone.

Scotty's body was returned to Springfield for burial. The funeral service took place at the same funeral home and chapel where his mother's service was held, where I had first met the eight-year-old Scotty standing next to her casket. Now, I stood next to his. Our lives had completed a sad, sad circle.

People came from all over the United States to pay their respects. Scotty died a lonely man and had no idea how many friends he had, or how many lives he'd touched. Standing room only, an overflow crowd poured from the chapel into the outside hallway. Interment was at the cemetery where his mother lay.

Expressions of sympathy along with many references to his infectious smile, humor, free spirit, incredible popularity, and success at a young age filled his online guest book. He was described as being a faithful friend, wise beyond his years, never putting himself on a pedestal, never taking himself too seriously, and always finding the good in every person.

At the funeral, his high school girlfriend of three years recalled how spending time with Scotty, running errands, and doing ordinary things were some of her greatest memories. With Scotty, the destination was never important. It was the journey. She viewed him as one of the greatest influences in her life, supporting and encouraging her even after they went their separate ways. They continued to stay in touch and kept up with each other's lives.

A young man approached me at the funeral, reminding me that we'd first met at Scotty's company, Prosperity Technical Services, Inc. The young man was Scotty's assistant, Joe.

After reminiscing about Scotty a few minutes, Joe shared a shocking revelation. He had talked Scotty out of suicide several times during the last few years.

Joe said Scotty's suicidal talk started during the summer of 2005. Sarah was living at her parents' house and refused to move back home. His loneliness, coupled with his difficulty holding a job, caused a great deal of anxiety and depression, and he started talking about taking his life.

"Sometimes when Scotty talked about suicide, he mentioned his mother," Joe said, "and her suicide weighed heavily on his mind. In addition," he continued, "Scotty was lost without Sarah."

"Several times," Joe recalled, "Scotty asked me to come to his house and take the hose so he would not use it to kill himself. I always did my best to cheer him up, and at times thought he was just lonely and would never take his life. His talk about suicide continued even after his move to Virginia Beach," Joe said, "although these conversations became less frequent. With hindsight," he continued, "I now feel badly I never shared this information with his family. I just assumed you knew."

After I disclosed this information to other family members, much to my surprise, Kathy acknowledged that she, too, had talked Scotty out of suicide during this same period.

"Scotty, how can you even think about such a thing?" Kathy had exclaimed when learning of his first attempt. "What about your family? We would be devastated."

"You would feel sad for awhile," he'd acknowledged, "just like we did when Mom committed suicide. But you'd get over it," he assured her.

Describing in detail his first unsuccessful attempt, he had told her of his disappointment when it failed, insinuating that he was a novice who would have to improve his skills if he was to succeed.

"I put the hose in the exhaust system and lay down in the backseat of the car for a long time, but nothing happened," he said. "After about an hour, I had to go inside to use the bathroom and tried again; still nothing happened."

The Oakton house had no garage. Scotty told Kathy how he'd placed a garbage can in front of the car exhaust so neighbors couldn't see the hose.

After this first attempt, Kathy made Scotty promise he would call her — day or night — the next time he felt suicidal. Instead, he had called after his second failed attempt. "I tried to use the hose again, but this time, my attempt was foiled because the automobile industry has gotten smarter and started installing mechanisms in exhaust systems to specifically prevent this from happening." Scotty had actually spent some time researching this information on the Internet.

Many times, he had purchased hoses and tossed them the next day so he would not be tempted to use them.

"I looked at hoses today," he casually told Kathy once, "but didn't buy them."

Once again, Virginia's restrictive law regarding involuntary commitment prohibited police involvement. This law, among the nation's most restrictive, is specific: The individual must be an "imminent danger to self" *when the report is made*. Since Kathy did not learn of her brother's two unsuccessful suicide attempts *until several weeks after* each attempt, the police would not get involved. In essence, what the police were saying was "Don't call us until your brother's suicide is successful at which time we'll respond with a body bag."

Tricia, Buddy, and Sarah were also aware of his attempts and lived in fear that Scotty might succeed someday. Kathy later explained that Scotty made her swear she would never tell me.

"There was nothing you could do to prevent another attempt, and I saw no reason to make you worry," she said.

I later learned that Sarah had received written instructions from Scotty during this period regarding his casket's color selection.

"If anything happens to me," his instructions read, "I want a blue casket like my Mom's."

When Tricia called our home on February 6, crying, asking to speak with George, I immediately knew Scotty was gone. All too familiar with the suicide rate for bipolar disorder, I, too, lived in fear he would take his life. Her call was one I never wanted to receive, but knew someday I would. The agony of having a loved one reach such a low point in life overwhelmed us all.

Guilt that perhaps we could have done more to prevent his death, together with all the "what ifs," plagued us all. For 13 long years, trying unsuccessfully to advocate for Scotty, we had watched his heartbreaking dissolution and decline with horror. As a family, I'm convinced we did all we could to help Scotty. The gross inadequacies of our mental health system failed to protect him when he could not protect himself. His blood is on their hands.

We love you, Scotty, and pray you have found the peace you have been searching for and that you are no longer lonely. You were so many good things to so many people, so much more than a young man trapped in a bipolar world. We hope that in the recesses of your heart and mind, you knew that.

EPILOGUE

Trapped in a body ravaged by irreversible damage from a mental illness that had gone untreated for long periods, Scotty found it increasingly difficult to cope. In just 13 years, he was transformed from a successful entrepreneur to an unemployed person. Upon his death, George and I were in the process of establishing a trust fund for Scotty so his siblings would not bear the long-term financial burden for his care.

Our broken mental health system bears the responsibility for Scotty's decline and death. Had the system let his wife and family force him to receive medical treatment each time he became ill, thus reducing the long periods he went untreated, he might be alive today. Instead, the system failed to protect him when he was too ill to protect himself.

Had the judge read and complied with Scotty's instructions in his Virginia Durable Power of Attorney for Health Care and given Sarah hope that she had the resources to get him treated and well again, I'm convinced she would have remained in the marriage. This vital document was drafted similarly to a Living Will that ensures proper health care treatment for those who are too ill to make their own decisions.

Scotty in his wisdom had the foresight to acknowledge that he suffered from bipolar disorder, and that when ill, he would refuse medication and treatment. He waived all rights to make his own health care decisions once a doctor certified he needed immediate mental health treatment and delegated this authority to six family members. He even acknowledged that when manic, he would do everything in his power to have the power of attorney declared invalid. He directed that his protests be ignored.

The laws in most states, and particularly Virginia, make it extraordinarily difficult for family members to get treatment for adults overcome by mental illness. Scotty knew the commitment laws not just in Virginia, but in every state along the East Coast. When manic, he became extremely accomplished at beating the system, never presenting as homicidal or suicidal. Released time and time again — forced to continue his pitiful existence — he lived in fear of his life in his untreated bipolar world.

There were times when I wanted to strangle the judges presiding at hearings, as well as the lawyers who represented Scotty. They let a severely mentally ill person outsmart them. Longing for a role reversal during those hearings, I wanted to be the judge and release the actual judge's mentally ill son. I wanted the judges to experience firsthand what it was like to constantly worry about the safety and future of a mentally ill son.

Bipolar disorder is a biological brain disorder that interferes with normal brain chemistry. Like diabetes, it can be controlled, but must be treated. It's a lifetime illness, but not a terminal illness. Many people with bipolar control their illness and have happy families and successful careers.

Some, like Scotty, however, suffer severe illness, yet they're permitted to go untreated for long periods, thus suffering further brain damage with each episode. The laws place so much emphasis on the civil rights of the mentally ill that the obstacles faced by families seeking proper treatment for adult relatives are ignored.

There was a time in this country when families could commit mentally ill relatives to mental hospitals for treatment. Unfortunately, some of those facilities became dumping grounds not only for the mentally ill, but also for people with physical disabilities and elderly people whose families no longer wanted to care for them. Some patients were badly mistreated by the staff and forgotten by their families.

When it became public knowledge that such deplorable conditions existed, a public outcry demanded changes in the system. Civil rights lawyers started filing class action lawsuits to close these hospitals, and states began discharging patients and passing laws to make it illegal to force treatment or medication on mentally ill people.

I applaud efforts to rid the country of those state-run asylums and their deplorable conditions. However, when passing laws to make it illegal to force treatment or medication on mentally ill people, lawmakers failed to consider people like Scotty. If you don't understand you're sick, how can you make rational decisions regarding your treatment? The answer is, you can't. The families of mentally ill people are the first to recognize that their loved ones are ill, but the law renders them helpless.

Scotty, in his untreated delusional, psychotic bipolar world, was a tragedy waiting to happen. Letting him roam the country under the pretense of protecting his civil rights is absurd. There must be balance in protecting the rights of severely mentally ill people and in acquiring much-needed treatment for them.

Always striving to learn more about Scotty's illness, I enrolled in a 12-week educational program that NAMI offered for family members of individuals with severe mental illness. The course began in January 2007 and ran for 12 consecutive Saturdays. The executive director for NAMI in Lee County, Florida, and the director of nursing at the Ruth Cooper Center for Behavioral Health Care in Fort Myers taught the course.

The program was specifically designed for family members of close relatives with mental illness. It was structured "1) to help them understand and support their ill relative while maintaining their own well-being, 2) to differentiate between what was in their control, when to back off, and when to become more involved, and 3) to show them how to manage the mental health system and advocate for their family member more effectively."

The class was limited to 20 people, all of whom were dealing with mental illness in their family. The instructors were excellent. We were told that the mental health system had failed us. Rather than letting ourselves become frustrated and angry, we were encouraged to confront the system's inequities by joining and promoting public advocacy groups and working together to bring about change.

The instructors explained that many families are torn apart by mental illness due to the confrontations and conflicts among family members trying to determine the best course of action. NAMI's feedback from the thousands of family members who'd taken this course was that they often felt they knew more about coping with mental illness than the professionals, because they had "on-the-job training" and had "graduated summa cum laude from the school of hard knocks."

The course underscored how insurance companies penalize the mentally ill by denying them adequate medical coverage. If you have heart, lung, or liver problems, your medical insurance typically pays for hospital expenses up to a million dollars. The same holds true if your brain malfunctions and your diagnosis is a brain tumor. However, if you have a brain disorder and your diagnosis is bipolar, your insurance may cover only a very limited hospital stay. In Scotty's case, his inpatient mental health care was a maximum of 30 days per year, contributing to his financial ruin.

I attended three sessions of the 12-week program before Scotty took his life. I did not return after his funeral. However, I highly recommend this course to all family members dealing with mental illness. NAMI is "a non-profit, grassroots, self-help, support and advocacy organization with more than 22,000 individual members working through more than 1,000 local and state affiliates. It is dedicated to the elimination of mental illness and to the improvement of the quality of life of those whose lives are affected by severe brain disorders. It provides support, education, referrals, resources, information, advocacy, and anti-stigma tools for those diagnosed with a mental illness. It does this through support groups, classes, resource rooms, presentations and membership meetings."

NAMI also offers a Peer-to-Peer Learning Program taught by a team of trained mentors who have personal experience in living with mental illness. Participants come away from this course with many resources, including a relapse prevention plan and survival skills for working with providers and the general public.

I tried repeatedly to persuade Scotty to attend this program in Virginia Beach, but he resisted each of my attempts. His sisters offered to attend the program with him, but he would have no part of it.

The consequences of non-treatment of the mentally ill are devastating. In the last two years, I have collected articles from our local newspaper describing violence by people with severe mental illness:

- A 19-year old bipolar man killed his psychiatrist during a visit.
- A bipolar mother cut off her baby's arm; police found her holding the knife and listening to a church hymn.
- A bipolar teenager stabbed his friend 50 times.
- A 76-year old bipolar man off his medications robbed a bank.
- A 28-year old bipolar man jumped from a moving airplane as it prepared to take off.
- A bipolar mother stabbed her seven-year-old daughter.
- A bipolar man repeatedly stabbed his mother.

- A bipolar mother snatched her two toddlers from their beds after smashing her car through a glass door at the house of their grandmother, who had custody of the children.
- A Florida air marshal shot a bipolar man off his meds claiming to have a bomb in his backpack after he left the plane but refused to submit to a search.
- A bipolar boy punched his teacher in the face.
- A bipolar man locked his mother in a closet for three days before a neighbor discovered her.
- A mentally ill mother stoned her two young sons because God told her to.
- A mentally ill mother smothered her nine-month-old twins, then went back to sleep.
- A bipolar man off his meds set fire to his cousin's house, killing five sleeping children.
- A depressed 23-year old mother hanged herself and her three children.
- A depressed mother drowned her five children in the family bathtub.
- A bipolar man shot six people during a psychotic episode; he thought they were aliens trying to abduct his five-year-old daughter.
- A bipolar man off his meds drove his car down a Florida airport runway alongside planes at up to 130 miles per hour before crashing.

I compiled this list in just two years, and it goes on and on.

The system on one hand denies mentally ill people treatment; on the other hand, it unleashes horror. April 16, 2007, a 23-year old Virginia Tech student gunned down 27 students and five faculty members before committing suicide. Yet, in December 2005, a Virginia judge had found this same young man to be mentally ill and an imminent danger to himself. He was ordered to receive outpatient treatment after being involuntarily committed overnight at a mental health center near Radford, Virginia. It's uncertain whether he ever returned for outpatient treatment.

This psychotic young man was able to purchase the guns he used in the massacre. His background check was clean. Was it considered a violation of this young man's rights to flag his name as a mentally impaired individual who shouldn't be allowed to purchase guns? What about the rights of those people he murdered?

During Scotty's fifth and final breakdown, when he began asking George to show him how to shoot a gun so he could exercise his right to bear arms and protect himself, we worried he might purchase a gun. We inquired how to register Scotty's name with the appropriate authorities and prevent this from happening; at least, we wanted to confirm that his name was already in the FBI database that licensed firearms dealers use to run background checks on prospective buyers. Due to privacy laws, we couldn't confirm that his name was in the database.

We must make state legislatures aware of the need to change laws pertaining to the treatment of mentally ill adults. One organization that works toward this goal is the Treatment Advocacy Center (TAC) in Arlington, Virginia.

TAC defines its objective as "a national nonprofit organization dedicated to eliminating legal and clinical barriers to timely and humane treatment for millions of Americans with severe brain disorders who are not receiving appropriate medical care." TAC "works on the national, state, and local levels to decrease homelessness, incarceration, suicide, victimization, violence, and other devastating consequences caused by lack of treatment."

Since TAC opened its doors in 1998, "treatment laws in 18 states have been improved." TAC "fights for those with the most severe mental illnesses who are left untreated because of deficient laws." Unlike many advocacy groups, "TAC does not accept funding from pharmaceutical companies or entities involved in the sale, marketing, or distribution of such products, which means their success hinges on donations."

In the aftermath of the Virginia Tech massacre, TAC led the campaign to convince the Virginia Legislature that the mental health system in its state, one of the most restrictive in the nation, was broken. Thanks to TAC and dedicated advocates from all across the state, the legislature did enact some modest changes in the law. The previous commitment language was changed from "imminent danger to self or others," to "the person will in the near future cause serious physical harm to himself or others as evidenced by recent behavior causing, attempting, or threatening harm."

This change falls short of what is needed, but it's a start.

My family's trials and tribulations throughout Scotty's illness were a grueling experience that at times brought us closer together. At other times, it tore us apart. We proved to be no exception to the general rule that when mental illness strikes a family, there are always some disagreements among family members as to the best course of action. In our case, there was criticism among family members about how others handled particular situations. Opposing views, hurt feelings, and friction resulted.

Scotty's struggle with bipolar disorder took a real toll on us. It was an extremely difficult and stressful time. During his 13-year illness, he was committed 14 times to 11 different hospitals. In addition to Virginia, he was committed to hospitals in the District of Columbia, North Carolina, South Carolina, and Florida. With each episode, we literally put our lives on hold for weeks on end, tracking Scotty and trying to get him treated. Tracking Scotty when manic, I might add, was no easy task, since his mania took him up and down the East Coast.

One thing we unanimously agreed upon was that we loved Scotty and hated that he had this illness. Kathy, Buddy, and Tricia all realize it was only the luck of the draw that Scotty inherited the bipolar gene and not them. Should the situation have been reversed and any one of us had Scotty's misfortune, he would have been there every step of the way, wanting and trying to help.

A SPECIAL NOTE

On August 22, 2008, another tragedy struck our family. We lost Buddy to alcohol-related bleeding and cirrhosis of the liver. He had struggled with alcoholism over the years, but after Scotty took his life, Buddy literally drank himself to death. We all saw it coming but could do nothing to help him. He refused to get professional treatment. He was 49 years old.

Research shows that alcoholism tends to run in families. His deceased biological mother also suffered from the disease.

Like his brother, Buddy, too, achieved a successful career in his mid-thirties before alcohol began to control his life. He leaves behind his former wife of 19 years and three beautiful daughters, ages 17, 11, and seven. Buddy requested that his ashes be buried at Scotty's gravesite.

Two sons, both in their forties, died tragic deaths a year and a half apart. It's overwhelming. The saddest thing for parents is to suffer a child's death. Predeceasing parents seems against the natural order. The pain of what happens to our children runs much deeper than what happens to us. Surely the order of recent events in our lives seems all wrong. Surely God had His reasons for doing this, reasons we may never understand. But surely, also, He will understand when we pray for needed rest from our family losses and for His loving protection over those of us who remain.

ABOUT THE AUTHOR

Dottie Pacharis is retired from a law firm in Washington, DC, and lives with her husband, George, also retired. They divide their time between Fort Myers Beach, Florida, and West River, Maryland. Since her son's battle with bipolar disorder, she has become an advocate for the mentally ill.

The Treatment Advocacy Center, Arlington, Virginia

A humane system is based on someone's need for treatment. A humane system protects those too sick to seek or accept care voluntarily. A humane system does not require someone to brandish a knife to get help or require them to hit rock bottom before they are lifted up again.

Uninformed calls to protect "civil rights" betray a profound misunderstanding of that term. There is nothing "civil" about leaving people lost to disease to live homeless on the streets, suffering rape, and victimization. There is nothing "right" about leaving someone untreated and psychotic, rendering them incapable of discerning whether they are attacking a CIA operative or their own mother.

Mentally ill individuals have a civil right to receive treatment, even when their brain disease precludes awareness of their illness. And the public has a civil right to be protected from potentially dangerous individuals. We are failing both the patients and the public.

This situation is an understandable overreaction to abuses of the past, when the mentally ill were confined too often and too long. But it's time for the pendulum to swing back to a more sensible middle.